Make and Break

A Play

Michael Frayn

Samuel French — London
New York – Sydney – Toronto – Hollywood

MAKE AND BREAK

First presented at the Lyric, Hammersmith on the 18th March, 1980. Subsequently presented by Michael Codron at the Theatre Royal, Haymarket, on the 24th April 1980 with the following cast of characters:

Tom Olley	James Grout
Frank Prosser	Peter Blythe
Colin Hewlett	Glyn Grain
Mrs Rogers	Prunella Scales
Verhaeren	Ray Edwards
Shariq	Ian Gray
Third Customer	Gary Fairhall
Ted Shaw	Anthony Roye
Anni	Catherine Neilson
John Garrard	Leonard Rossiter
Dr Horvath	David Graham
Peter Davis	Donald Morley
Doctor	Paul Gregory

The Play directed by Michael Blakemore

Setting by Michael Annals

The action takes place on an exhibition stand at a trade fair

Time—the present

ACT I

An exhibition stand at a trade fair

The stand is displaying a partitioning system intended for use in offices and other public buildings. The system consists of what appears to be completely solid walling, finished in veneered panels. But sections of the wall can be moved and turned into new positions. The system includes a number of doors

Signs announce:

MODUS—the complete wall system for all your walling problems
MODUS—das vollständige Wandsystem für alle Ihre Wand-probleme
MODUS brings you the TOTAL INTERNAL ENVIRONMENT
MODUS—die totale Innere Umwelt!
MODUS—the only integrated walling and Bürolandschaft system
MODUS—das einzige integrierte Wand—und Bürolandschaft-system

The stand has been set up in the sitting-room of a large hotel suite, so that it forms a kind of room within a room, complete with a desk for the sales staff and a drinks table. The suite has a door giving access to the corridor, and another opening into a bedroom

Four members of the Modus sales force are on the stand: Olley, the Sales Director, mid-fifties; Prosser, the Publicity Manager, forty; Hewlett, one of the reps, mid-twenties; and Mrs Rogers, Olley's secretary, forty. There are also three customers: Verhaeren, who is Belgian, and who is being dealt with by Olley; Shariq, an Arab businessman, who is being seen to by Prosser; and a Third Customer, of Far Eastern appearance, who is with Hewlett

Mrs Rogers is dealing with the telephone, the paperwork, and keeping the customers' glasses filled. Olley, Prosser and Hewlett are all talking to their respective customers simultaneously

Olley Now it all depends what you're looking for. I can quote you thirty-five pounds a metre delivered. What's that in

Belgian francs? —sixty francs to the pound, that's sixty times thirty-five—brain's not working at the end of the day—well, let's say roughly two thousand francs a metre. Fine—if you can get away with a flaxboard core and semi-solid doors . . .

Prosser Now you want full demountability and you want full recoverability. But you don't want to end up with some kind of temporary accommodation for homeless families. Because you've looked at some of those demountable partitions on the floor down there, and you think a demountable partition's going to look demountable and feel demountable . . .

Hewlett Now as far as facings go, we can supply a standard hardboard facing for site finishing. Or, if you want a painted wood finish, we can do a rotary-cut birch at a very competitive price. Or we can supply ex-stock all the hardwood veneers you can see on the stand here, plus a number of others you don't. If you look through the catalogue, you'll see we are offering, ex-stock . . .

There is a distant explosion. Everyone stops for an instant, and turns his head to listen. Then business at once resumes. As the conversations continue—consecutively, not simultaneously, from this point on—the three salesmen and their customers appear and disappear through the doors in the stand, or emerge and become audible as the movement of the movable sections is demonstrated

Olley And for that price you're getting a fire-rated wall, mind, a thirty-minute fire wall that you can put in place with one hand . . .

Hewlett A full range of hardwood veneers—abura, afrormosia, agba, bird's eye maple . . .

Prosser Where were we? Oh yes—you think, right, a demountable partition's going to look demountable and feel demountable . . .

Olley But if you want a sixty-minute fire wall, then you've got to go to plasterboard and steel . . .

Hewlett . . . koto, limba, mansonia, okume, paldao, and zebrano . . .

Prosser Well, just forget partitions. Partitions are things that rattle when you slam the door. These are *walls*. This is a *wall system*. Fully demountable, fully adjustable walls combined with a range of fully uniform finishes for your load-bearing elements. Movable solid walls. You can't see where the structural element stops and the movable element starts until I unlock it and turn it . . .

Olley . . . not cheap, no one's saying it's cheap, but for that price you're getting steel, you're getting a sixty-minute fire wall. In fact it's rated sixty/sixty—sixty minutes stability and sixty minutes integrity . . .

Mrs Rogers Whisky and soda, wasn't it, Mr Verhaeren?

Verhaeren (*to Mrs Rogers*) Very kind of you. (*To Olley*) But I think on the Zwijndrecht site our big problem will be sound transmission.

Olley Sound transmission? This core will give you a sound reduction of forty-seven decibels! You won't get more than forty-five decibels with hundred-mil brickwork! And look, I just unlock it and turn it . . .

Hewlett . . . the standard core is inert European flaxboard, but of course if the overriding consideration is the floor loading, then you're going to choose extruded chipboard as your core option . . .

Prosser . . . bird's eye maple, Columbian pine, Honduras mahogany, idigbo, iroko, koto, limba, mansonia . . .

Olley . . . and the point is that this is a piece of factory-made precision engineering . . .

Mrs Rogers Here you are, Mr Verhaeren—whisky and soda.

Verhaeren Very kind.

Olley You can't get this standard of workmanship from the chippies on the site. You can't work to these tolerances in on-site conditions . . .

Shariq Now, on the question of delivery dates.

Prosser In Abu Dhabi? Well, we're promising ten weeks anywhere in Western Europe, but for the Gulf, I'll have to consult our shippers.

Mrs Rogers (*to Shariq*) Let me just top up your lemon squash.

Shariq Thank you.

Prosser So if I could just put your name and the address of your company down in our book . . .

Shariq I'll give you my card . . .

Olley . . . mansonia, okoume, paldao, or zebrano, or if you're going to paint it then specify plain birch. The rotary cut is the cheapest, of course, but if you want a clear finish you might find you'd rather go for the quarter cut, which is the straight grain showing the most figuring, or the crown cut, which shows off the heart features of the wood . . .

Hewlett I mean, *is* floor loading a consideration?

The Third Customer laughs charmingly

The floor loading—is it important . . .? *Floor loading* . . . Floor . . . (*He demonstrates the floor*)

The Customer laughs

Excuse me, may I ask what language exactly . . .?

Customer Oh, yes.

Hewlett Which? Language. Which language?

Customer Oh, please, yes.

Mrs Rogers Another?

Customer Thank you, yes.

Hewlett Just a moment—we've got a lot of stuff translated into French and German . . .

Prosser . . . No, just between ourselves, we think we've got a winner here. That's why we've only got a token display down there in the hall with the rest of them. We reckon if people are interested they'll come back here to the hotel and have a drink and take a good hard look at what we've got to offer . . .

Olley . . . No, I'll be frank with you. The point as far as *you're* concerned is lower site costs, because two semi-skilled blokes can install a twenty-metre run of this stuff complete—facings on and doors hung—in two to three hours. But the point of the system as far as *we're* concerned—and I'll be quite frank— is the bigger the unit we sell you, the bigger the profit margin . . .

Hewlett (*with leaflets*) . . . We've got this one in Spanish.

Customer Thank you.

Hewlett Or we can do Swedish.

Customer Thank you.

Mrs Rogers Dry Martini.

Customer Thank you.

Hewlett Anyway, if I can just have your name and address, I'll get something sent off. Through here . . . What's your name?

Olley . . . because I'll be frank with you—we're really a door firm . . .

Prosser . . . doors—that's what we're known for . . .

Olley That used to be our entire trade—doors.
Prosser Ajax Doors—ask anyone in the British building trade.
Olley Then we all went into door sets.
Prosser Then we pioneered the door set.
Olley Lower fixing costs.
Prosser Meet the new fire regulations.
Olley But really to sell you a frame as well as a door.
Prosser Now we're extending the advantages of the door set to
   the entire wall area.
Olley Come back in two years time and we'll sell you the floor
   and ceiling as well.
Prosser Anyway, you've got my card . . .
Olley You've got all the bumph . . .
Hewlett You've got my card . . . *Card* . . .

The Third Customer laughs

   Hewlett sees him out and returns

Prosser I'm not giving away any secrets when I tell you we've
   got a slump in the building trade at home. We've come over
   here to Frankfurt because we need the business.

*There is a second explosion. Once again heads briefly turn, and
then the conversation resumes*

   No, we've come to exhibit at a big international fair because
   we're really serious, believe me. So there won't be any trouble
   about delivery dates, I'll give you my word on that.
Olley . . . Ah, well, now, I'm not the expert on that side of the
   business. For that we'll have to consult Mr Prosser, our
   Publicity Manager . . . Frank . . . excuse me . . . Can I interrupt
   a minute?
Prosser Hold on, Tom . . . (*To Shariq*) Anyway, look, you've got
   the catalogue, you've got the price-list. What else can we give
   you?
Olley (*to Hewlett*) Beauty you've got there.
Hewlett I think he was quite interested in the extruded chip-
   board. (*He sits*)
Olley Don't worry. All good practice.
Prosser Right, then, Tom. What's the problem? (*To Hewlett*)
   My word, Colin, you do pick 'em, don't you?

Olley Frank, this is Mr Verhaeren.

Prosser How do you do, Mr Verhaeren?

Olley Mr Verhaeren's building two big leisure complexes in the Antwerp area—

Prosser Yes, I've been reading about it.

Olley —and he wants to go out this evening and test his fire-resistance.

Prosser Fire-resistance?

Verhaeren laughs

Olley Take in a bit of the local night-life. I told him you're the firm's expert on wining and dining.

Prosser Leave it to me, Mr Verhaeren. I've got all the technical data on Frankfurt on the desk here. If you want something really outrageous there's always *Rheingold* at the Opera House.

Olley (*to Shariq*) Do you mind? Let me at least freshen up that lemon squash for you . . .

Shaw enters. He is in his fifties, and wears his glasses some way down his nose to make clear his benevolent, patriarchal nature

Hewlett rises to deal with him

Hewlett Good afternoon. Can I help you at all? Or are you just looking round? Do you speak English?

Shaw (*staring*) Well, bless my old cotton socks. They've asked me some damn funny questions since I've been here, but no-one's asked me that.

Hewlett Oh, sorry. Only . . .

Shaw What's your name, then?

Hewlett Hewlett. Colin Hewlett.

Shaw (*looking at Hewlett's lapel badge*) Hewlett. Oh yes. Mr Hewlett. How are you, Mr Hewlett?

Hewlett Fine. Fine. And you're . . .? (*He tries to see Shaw's lapel badge*)

Shaw I'm fine too, Mr Hewlett. *You* speak English, do you, Mr Hewlett?

Hewlett Yes, yes . . .

Shaw We shall get along very well then.

Hewlett I'm sorry. It's just that . . .

Shaw They've left you in charge of this impressive display, have they, Mr Hewlett?

Hewlett Well, I think the others are just . . .

Shaw Round the back?

Hewlett Yes, so if I can . . .

Shaw They'll rot their livers, Mr Hewlett.

Hewlett I don't know whether you've any particular—

Shaw Well, as long as there's one of the party still fit to drive.

Hewlett —any particular problems or queries you'd got in mind, or whether . . .

Shaw As long as there's one member of the firm still sober enough to sell the partitions.

Hewlett Ah, well now, that's rather interesting, because as a matter of fact these aren't partitions. This is a wall system—a fully integrated wall system.

Shaw Is it indeed?

Hewlett Yes, because what this system offers you is a complete internal environment.

Mrs Rogers (*bringing a drink*) Whisky, is it, Mr Shaw?

Shaw That's my lass.

Hewlett All right, it comes as fully demountable, fully recoverable units that can be unlocked and shifted in a matter of seconds. But it also comes in the form of fully uniform finishes for your load-bearing walls.

Shaw Fully uniform are they?

Hewlett Fully uniform.

Shaw You're not going to tell me, are you, Mr Hewlett, that these units have a core of inert European flaxboard?

Hewlett Inert European flaxboard, yes.

Mrs Rogers I think Mr Olley is free to see you now, Mr Shaw.

Olley (*seeing Shariq out*) Anyway, you've got my card . . .

Hewlett Or where the floor-loading is the overriding consideration, extruded chipboard.

Shariq exits

Mrs Rogers draws Olley's attention to Shaw. Olley watches him and Hewlett

Or if you have a fire-rating problem, then the answer is our Firemode range in plasterboard and steel, which will give you sixty/sixty fire resistance, and incidentally a sound attenuation of around forty-seven decibels . . .

Shaw (*glancing at Olley*) Which is more than you get from the traditional brick wall.

Hewlett Which is more than you get from the traditional brick wall.

Shaw Got your order-book?

Hewlett Beg your pardon?

Shaw Take an order, can you?

Hewlett An order? Yes—yes ...

Shaw Handle thirty thousand square feet?

Hewlett Thirty thousand ...? Yes—yes ...

Shaw Where's your book, then?

Hewlett turns to fetch his book and sees Olley

Hewlett The book, the book ...

Olley Speaks English, does he, this one?

Hewlett Yes, quick, where's the book?

Olley (*shaking hands with Shaw*) I see you're in form, then, Mr Shaw.

Shaw You've got a good one here, Tom.

Olley Not his day. Is it, Colin?

Shaw No, he almost sold it to me. Thirty thousand square feet. I don't know what of.

Olley Colin, this is Mr Shaw. Mr Shaw's the managing director of Securex.

Hewlett I'm sorry, I thought you were ...

Olley Heard of Securex, have you, Colin?

Hewlett Yes, I ...

Shaw One of the Group, Mr Hewlett, one of the Group.

Hewlett Yes, I ...

Shaw Took one look at me, thought I was Japanese.

Hewlett No, I ...

Shaw What's your territory, then, Mr Hewlett?

Hewlett South-West.

Olley Out of Bristol.

Shaw I'll bet you can't get the orders out of the warehouse fast enough to keep up with him.

Olley He's all right.

Shaw Colin, is it? You'll do, Colin, you'll do.

Olley So how can we help you, Mr Shaw?

Shaw Oh, just looking in, pick up a few tips on how to do it. All right for some, isn't it, relaxing in a suite at the best hotel. Some of us less fortunate mortals are sweating it out down there in the hall, crying our wares in the market-place.

Olley We've got a stand down there, too, you know.

Shaw What, ten by ten? One girl and three pieces of Marler-Haley? Trust old John—tuck you away up here and save himself fourteen and sevenpence.

Prosser All right, then, Mr Verhaeren. Eight o'clock at your hotel.

Olley Excuse me, Mr Shaw. (*To Verhaeren*) All fixed up for tonight?

Verhaeren Paint the town red. Correct?

Prosser Red, blue, primrose yellow—you name it—we'll paint it.

Verhaeren And tomorrow—nine o'clock, here, and we talk business.

Olley Nine o'clock.

Prosser Red, blue; abura, afrormosia, agba, bird's eye maple . . .

Verhaeren What?

Prosser The town. Any finish the customer wants.

Verhaeren exits in a jovial mood

Shit.

Olley What?

Prosser I'd got a ticket for the Opera. It's *Rheingold*.

Shaw You'll just have to keep your mind on the building trade instead.

Prosser Hello, Mr Shaw. (*Shaking hands*) The building trade? That's what *Rheingold*'s all about! They build bloody Valhalla!

Shaw Frank could have sold them some partitions.

Olley Yes, well, Verhaeren's building *two* bloody Valhallas.

Prosser Bloody Belgians.

Shaw Still binding away, Frank? Used to work for me. Know that, Colin? (*To Prosser*) Why you wanted to come and work for some tin-pot little firm like this, sell all this rubbish. I was just saying to Tom, John's trying to save a few quid, is he, tucking you all away up here? Why you want to come and work for a miserable old mule like John . . . Can you hear me, John? Where is he? Is he over?

Olley Coming tomorrow.

Shaw Recognize him, will you, Colin? Your managing director?

Hewlett Yes.

Shaw Don't go selling the partitions to him.

Hewlett No.

Shaw So it's tomorrow the bomb falls. Do a cheap excursion on Wednesdays, do they? I'll tell you what, though—I shouldn't all line up at the airport to meet him, because if old John says he's coming tomorrow you can be sure of one thing—it won't be tomorrow, it'll be the day after. Or else it'll be yesterday. Wasn't yesterday, was it?

Olley You want to see him, do you, Mr Shaw? It's really him you're looking for?

Anni enters. She is German, and in her early twenties

Shaw Want to see John? Why should anyone want to see an ugly old monkey like John? I've come to see Anni. (*He puts his arm round her*)

Anni You're not all still working?

Shaw Of course we're working. We're English. We're not idle Germans, like you.

Anni It's after six o'clock! Everyone sit down! Everyone start resting and enjoying! You poor tired businessmen!

Shaw (*putting his arm round her*) I could just eat you for supper, do you know that?

Prosser You know Mr Shaw, do you, Anni?

Anni I know Mr Shaw. Sit down! Why is everyone standing up? You like work, or something? I know—I'll bring you all a drink. No, no—you were drinking all day. Drinking is working. I'll get some coffee.

Prosser Coffee, yes!

Olley Coffee for me.

Mrs Rogers Coffee? I'll make the coffee.

Anni Sit down!

Mrs Rogers If people want coffee, I can perfectly well make coffee.

Anni makes coffee

Anni (*to Olley*) You got Mr Shariq, I suppose?

Olley That was the Arab gentleman?

Prosser Hospital job. Abu Dhabi. Twenty thousand pounds worth, I should think, to someone.

Anni Then there was some man from some place—I'm sorry, I couldn't get his name. I couldn't make him understand not one word.

Hewlett We got him.

Anni I received some questions.

Prosser Inquiries.

Anni Inquiries. I wrote them all down in the book.

Olley Anything interesting?

Anni Yes, quite interesting. What do I do in the evening? How much rent do I pay? Am I some kind of Communist?

Prosser Who was this?

Anni Oh, some crazy man. I must telephone. Did you hear those explosions?

Olley Yes, what were they?

Prosser The whole stand shook.

Anni I don't know. (*Dialling*) Some people, I suppose, were exploding some things. Some shops, some U-Bahn station, I don't know.

Mrs Rogers sits and works at the small table behind the display stand

Olley What, you mean terrorists?

Anni Some crazy people.

Shaw Same everywhere these days. What a world.

Anni Why? What does it matter? Plenty of shops. Plenty of things for exploding. (*Into the telephone*) *Du Scheisskerl!* ... *Was machst du die ganze Zeit?* ... *Ich klingle schon seit einer halben Stunde* ...

Shaw (*wistfully*) Doesn't give a damn, does she?

Prosser Why should she? She's a student. Doing some kind of law degree. Week's work with us at the fair, and she's made enough to live on for a month.

Shaw Not a tuppenny damn about any of us.

They watch her. She laughs at something on the telephone

Olley I suppose they're pals of hers letting off the bomb, are they?

Shaw Letting off a few bombs herself, I shouldn't wonder. Look at her. Little anarchist you've got there, Tom.

Olley Not all alike, you know, these students.

Shaw Little terrorist—look at her. Well, why not? Get to my age and you wouldn't mind seeing half of it go up in smoke. Anyway, some of us have work to do, some of us have products to sell. Take care, then, Tom.

Olley You, too, Mr Shaw.

Shaw Look after yourself, Frank. Oh, and Davis found his way up here all right, did he?

Olley I beg your pardon?

Shaw Davis.

Olley Davis?

Prosser What, our Davis?

Shaw He did find you?

Olley How do you mean, find us?

Shaw I thought he might have been looking for you.

Olley What, here? In Frankfurt?

Prosser He's in New York this week.

Shaw Well, then, I've got news for you gentlemen.

Olley Good God. We haven't . . . ?

Prosser No—no . . .

Olley Have you, Colin?

Hewlett Who is this? Sorry.

Prosser Peter Davis.

Olley Our new group managing director.

Prosser Our new whizz-kid.

Hewlett *I* haven't seen him.

Olley (*to Shaw*) What would he be doing in Frankfurt?

Shaw That's what *I'd* like to know.

Prosser You've seen him, have you?

Shaw He hasn't been near me. I thought it might have been you lot he was favouring. I thought he and John might have been having little chats.

Olley No, no. No Peter Davis—no John.

Shaw I'll believe you; thousands wouldn't. That's all I wanted to find out. Knew I was after something, didn't you? Well, now you can relax and drink your coffee in peace—I'm there at last. Got my little ways, haven't I, Frank? Always take my time. Frank'll tell you. Nice to meet you, Colin. And I should be leaving with your card in my pocket, you see.

Hewlett Oh—yes—I . . .

Shaw Don't worry, Colin. You'll learn. Look after yourselves, then.

Olley And you, Mr Shaw.

Shaw Just say ta-ta to Anni. (*He kisses her free ear*) Don't forget—back of the bandstand at eight o'clock ... (*To the others, apropos Mrs Rogers*) Oh—a bit of a look from the lady there. (*To Mrs Rogers*) Never mind, my sweetheart, we'll go rock-and-rolling together another night.

Shaw exits

Prosser Bloody old humbug.

Olley What was all that in aid of?

Prosser Always on the snuffle.

Olley I wish he'd keep his fingers off our Anni.

Prosser Always on the wink. Always on the hug and squeeze. Always slipping it to you out of the back of the hand. And in fact they're taking that firm to pieces all around him. Ridiculous, really. They make security fencing—they can't keep their own stocks secure! When I was there—you won't believe this— they put in dogs to stop the thieving and what happened?— someone walked off with all the dogs' bloody food—ten cases of bloody dog meat! Security fencing?—They couldn't sell a rope to a drowning man. No dividend again this year.

Olley He thinks Peter Davis and John are up to something behind his back.

Prosser The whole world's going on behind his back.

Anni (*into the telephone*) Schuss. (*She puts the telephone down*) You're not working again? I told you to sit down! Sit, sit, sit!

Olley Yes, what *are* we standing up for? We've been standing up all day. (*He sits*) Ah.

Anni Oh, it's so good to hear this sound! (*To Prosser and Hewlett*) Now you, please.

Prosser I've been saving it up.

Prosser and Hewlett sit. Mrs Rogers comes to the desk and starts to tidy it and empty ashtrays

Ah.

Anni It's like the sound of making love.

Prosser Oh, tell us more.

Anni I'll make some more coffee. (*She does so*)

Hewlett Gets you in the stomach, doesn't it?

Prosser Just over the kidneys, me.

Olley It's my smiling muscles.

Prosser I'll never get my face straight again.

Olley Inert European flaxboard. I'll be saying it in my sleep.

Prosser Inert European flaxboard.

Olley Inert European flaxboard.

Prosser I'll tell you what, though. It's lovely just sitting here and saying it and not meaning it.

Olley Inert European flaxboard. Yes, it is.

Prosser Inert European flaxboard. It's very soothing.

Olley No, it's a wonderful thing, work.

Prosser If it wasn't for work you'd never have the pleasure of stopping.

Olley Colin's looking very thoughtful about all this.

Hewlett Sorry? No, I was just wondering what Sandra's doing. (*He looks at his watch*) Bathing the kids, I expect. Whole bathroom awash. Driving her out of her mind.

Olley That's the trouble with stopping work. You start worrying.

Hewlett No, I was just wondering. Actually, Jonathan's probably not having a bath tonight. He was starting a cold on Sunday.

Anni (*bringing the coffee*) What's this? Everyone's so stiff, everyone's behaving so proper. I don't call this relaxing. (*She puts the coffee down, and sets to work on Olley*) Lean back.

Olley I'm fine.

Anni Come on. Undo your tie.

Olley I don't want my tie undone.

Anni (*setting a chair*) Feet here.

Olley I don't want my feet there!

Anni I'm putting your feet here!

Prosser She'll have you in the bath in a minute, Tom, like Colin's kids.

Olley What's happening?

Anni I'm taking your shoes off.

Prosser Isn't she a honey?

Olley I don't know what she is.

Anni Other foot.

Prosser Hold on to your trousers, Tom.

Olley You're shocking Mrs Rogers.
Prosser Look at him, though! He loves it, he loves it!
Anni There! Isn't that better?
Olley No.

Anni kisses Olley

Prosser Oh, and a kiss as well!
Olley (*pleased*) Oh, bloody hell!
Anni (*to Prosser*) Now you.
Prosser Certainly, my love. First the kiss.
Anni First the shoes. (*She takes off his shoes*)
Prosser Oh, but that's lovely—someone picking up your feet for
    you.
Olley That's what I call service—being handed your own feet.
Prosser You know what I'd like to be in my next incarnation?—
    a ventriloquist's dummy. Somebody else moving my jaw up
    and down. Somebody else thinking the thoughts. I could really
    sit back and enjoy that. (*To Anni*) Don't forget the tie, love.
Anni (*loosening his tie*) Oh, this one is a very good patient.
Olley Don't worry, Colin—you'll get your turn in a minute.
Hewlett (*recollecting himself*) Sorry?
Prosser Not brooding about his family again, is he?
Hewlett No, I was just thinking, when I'm away overnight at
    home I usually give Sandra a ring about seven. See if they went
    to bed all right.
Prosser How old are they?
Hewlett Mark's four, Jonathan's nineteen months.
Prosser Don't often stay out all night yet, do they?
Anni No, that's good to think about his family. (*She kisses
    Hewlett*)
Prosser Don't do that!
Anni Not?
Prosser He's religious.
Anni Yes? (*She steps back from him, hands off*)
Prosser Yes! He saves people's souls! They've just had some big
    do in tents down in Exeter. How many souls did you save
    down there, Colin?
Olley Dry up, Frank. We all know you're a heathen.
Hewlett No, that's all right. I don't mind.

Anni He doesn't mind. (*She puts Hewlett's feet up and undoes the laces*)

Hewlett (*trying to stop her*) No—thank you—no . . .

Olley (*reasonably but firmly*) Anni—Anni . . .

Anni (*desisting*) Not?

Hewlett I mean we had over a thousand people coming forward.

Prosser That firm orders, though, or just inquiries?

Olley (*warning*) Frank . . .

Prosser He doesn't mind talking about it.

Olley I do, though. Hey, what about Mrs Rogers? Why hasn't she got her feet up?

Anni and Prosser turn their attention to Mrs Rogers, who is still tidying the stand. Hewlett is left to tie up his shoes

Anni (*to Mrs Rogers*) Stop! Stop! Stop!

Prosser Not going to take Mrs R's shoes off, is she?

Olley Does she do ladies?

Anni Sit down, please!

Mrs Rogers I think I'll just finish this, thank you, Miss Friedrich. Mr Garrard won't be very pleased if he arrives tomorrow and finds overflowing ashtrays everywhere.

Anni If who arrives tomorrow?

Prosser Mr Garrard.

Olley The Managing Director.

Prosser Now there's a real challenge for Anni!

Anni What? What?

Olley (*laughing*) Yes, you won't get John's shoes off, I'll tell you that.

Anni Why? He's another religious?

Olley and Prosser laugh

Olley No, he's not a religious.

Prosser Nothing in his head but walls and doors.

Olley I wouldn't say that. I'm the one who thinks about walls and doors.

Prosser True. What he cares about is profits.

Mrs Rogers Mr Garrard? He doesn't care twopence about money.

Olley She's right, you know. He doesn't.

Olley and Prosser laugh again

Anni So what's funny about this man?
Prosser Tell her, Tom. You've known him for thirty years.
Olley Thirty-two.
Prosser Go on, then.

Olley just laughs and shakes his head

Anni What? What? What?
Prosser I'll tell you the first thing he'll do when he walks in here. He'll rearrange that display. Fiddle, fiddle, fiddle, while he goes on about the emptiness of the order book and the price of paper-clips.
Olley Never stops, that's the thing about John.
Prosser We shan't be sitting around in our socks once he's arrived.
Olley You get John Garrard to put his feet up for five minutes, Anni. Be a public blessing.
Prosser (*grinning*) What do you bet she gets his shoes off?
Olley I'll bet you five pounds she *doesn't*.
Anni Five pounds? For me? If I get his shoes off?
Prosser No, for me. The bet's with me.
Olley Ten pounds, if you like.
Prosser All right.
Anni And what do *I* get?
Prosser You get a kiss from me. And half my winnings.
Anni Five pounds?
Prosser Five pounds.
Anni All right.
Prosser Got one deal set up here, anyway. And you're coming out tonight with me and Mr Verhaeren?
Olley She's coming out with me and Mr Goetz. Aren't you, my dear?
Anni No, tonight I must make something with some people. So you know what I'm going to do now?
Prosser Shoot up into the sky and burst out in coloured stars.
Anni I'm going to take a shower. Is that OK?
Prosser As long as you don't take it to extremes.
Anni What?
Olley Take it, take it.

Anni exits into the bedroom

Prosser smiles

Hewlett As a matter of fact three hundred and forty of them declared.

Prosser (*stopping smiling*) I beg your pardon?

Hewlett Three hundred and forty of the people who came forward.

Prosser Yes?

Hewlett Declared for Christ.

Prosser Oh.

Hewlett You were asking about it.

Prosser So I was. (*He begins to smile again*) Anni, though. "I must make something with some people." *Make* something!

Olley Make trouble.

Prosser (*smiling*) Make trouble for someone.

Olley Make a few explosions.

Prosser Oh, Ted Shaw wouldn't know an anarchist from an anabaptist.

Olley I can see Mrs Rogers thinks she's going to blow us all up.

Mrs Rogers She shouldn't be using the shower.

Olley gazes at her

Well, she shouldn't.

Olley (*turning to Prosser*) Ten years now, is it, since Mrs Rogers did me the honour of becoming my secretary?

Mrs Rogers You know perfectly well she shouldn't.

Olley But still she continues to amaze me.

Mrs Rogers It's Mr Garrard's shower.

Prosser Don't be embarrassed, Colin. They go on like this all the time.

Mrs Rogers This is Mr Garrard's suite. It's booked in his name. That's his bedroom and that's his bathroom.

Olley But he's not here, Mrs Rogers, my precious! And we are!

Mrs Rogers We have the use of the sitting-room. But the bedroom and the bathroom are his.

Olley But my sweet lovely woman, we all use the bathroom! *I* use the bathroom! *You* use the bathroom!

Mrs Rogers We don't use the shower. You wouldn't use the shower. Mr Prosser wouldn't use the shower.

Prosser (*to Hewlett*) They're devoted to each other, really.

Olley (*to Prosser*) No, but it's amazing the way her mind works.
Mrs Rogers I simply think it's a bit odd that she can come waltzing in here and just take the whole place over.
Olley Oh, it's not the shower she's worried about.
Mrs Rogers Well, it is ridiculous, you know, to see her making fools of you all. Because that's what she's doing. She's simply showing she can twist you round her finger.
Olley John won't be worried about the shower. I'll tell you what he cares about. It's not money. It's not the product. I've watched John in action now for thirty-two years, and I'll tell you what he cares about . . .

Garrard enters. Like Olley, he is in his mid-fifties. He is carrying an overnight bag

Everyone gazes at him in astonishment. But he ignores them. He is absorbed in the door by which he has entered. He pushes it to, and watches it close. Then he opens it and watches it close again

Mrs Rogers (*rising*) Hello, Mr Garrard.

Hewlett gets to his feet. Olley and Prosser struggle to theirs

Hewlett Mr Garrard . . .
Prosser Mr Garrard . . .
Olley John . . . I thought it was tomorrow?
Prosser I was going to meet you at the airport—I'd booked a car . . .

They put their feet back into their shoes. But Garrard is still absorbed in the operation of the door

Garrard Chair.
Olley What?
Garrard Chair, chair.

Prosser fetches a chair. Garrard puts down his bags, raps on the door in a couple of different places, then climbs on to the chair and examines the top edge of the door

Olley What, a semi-solid, is it? (*He raps*) No, softwood laminate?
Garrard When did they get this contract, then?
Olley Who?

Garrard Parker Matthews. This is a Parker Matthews door. (*He looks round the room*) Repro job, was it?

Olley I don't know, I'm afraid, John.

Garrard Done, what, five years ago? How long have Parker been into the German market?

Olley Just about five years, I think. Isn't it, Frank?

Prosser I don't know.

Garrard Parker Matthews throughout, is it? Restaurant? Ballroom?

Olley I have to confess, John, I haven't looked.

Garrard (*getting off the chair*) What about Verhaeren? Has he come through?

Olley Verhaeren? Frank's taking him out to dinner tonight . . .

Garrard But nothing yet?

Olley Nothing definite. I'm dining with a contractor who's doing a lot of the Westphalia schools programme.

Garrard Uh-huh. No messages from London?

Olley No. Colin here thought he'd got an order for thirty thousand square feet, but it just turned out to be Ted Shaw playing the fool.

Garrard Uh-huh.

Olley You remember Colin Hewlett, don't you? Bristol office.

Garrard Yes, yes. But what about the Arabs?

Olley Lot of interest. *Lot* of interest.

Prosser If you just run your eye over the inquiries book.

Olley Oh, the fallout from this fair is going to be fantastic. And we've got the Libyan contract in the bag.

Garrard That was last week. What did Ted Shaw want?

Prosser Oh, he was just on the snuffle.

Garrard Uh-huh. How many hotels are there in this group?

Olley I've no idea.

Garrard I wonder if Parker Matthews got the contract for the whole chain.

Prosser I'll make some inquiries, if you're interested.

Garrard Should have had a stunt, shouldn't we.

Olley A stunt?

Garrard Ridgways had got a great crowd round their flame-thrower stunt.

Prosser Oh, you had a look at the exhibition, did you, Mr Garrard?

Olley What time did you arrive?

Garrard Thirty people. I counted them. Thirty-one, including me.

Olley Still, I don't think Ridgways are selling anything.

Garrard They've just sold three hundred thousand pounds' worth to the Nigerian government.

Olley News to me.

Prosser Where did you hear that, Mr Garrard?

Garrard (*looking at his watch*) Got someone coming in fifteen minutes. Hungarian. (*He takes out a visiting-card*) Horvath. Dr Horvath. Architect. Specifying for this new international conference centre the Hungarians are building on Lake Balaton.

Olley Just ran into this bloke at the exhibition, did you, John?

Prosser Doesn't waste much time, does he, Tom?

Garrard This could be very important for us. Get our products in at this international conference centre, and we could be in right the way across Eastern Europe ... At the exhibition? No, in the taxi from the airport. Let's see—he comes in, and I'm sitting at the table talking to Tom. Colin gets up and meets him at the door. Now where's Frank going to be ...?

Prosser I could be on the display.

Olley Sticky, is he, this bloke? One of these Communist officials?

Garrard Frank could be by the window. Let's get these chairs shifted round, make them look a bit more natural.

Olley Very peaceful it was before you arrived, John.

Garrard He comes in here, it looks as if we're all waiting for him. And that display ... (*He gazes at it*)

Prosser catches Olley's eye. Olley grins. Prosser makes signs to Hewlett, pointing to Garrard and the display. Garrard suddenly turns on Prosser

So what are you telling me?

Prosser What?

Garrard You're telling me we've got nothing?

Prosser Not yet, no.

Olley We're not selling brushes, John.

Garrard Better call a press conference tomorrow and announce the Libyan contract. Be something. Show some sign of life.

Prosser Right. But you were just going to say something about the display.

Garrard (*gazing absently at the display*) No good just sitting up here and doing nothing. Lot of little furry animals gone to sleep for the winter . . . So then Tom can show him the stuff. I'll pour him a drink. No, we'll all have a drink. Talk, talk, talk. Then Tom says why don't you have a look at the stuff since you're here . . . (*He looks at his watch*) Ten minutes. I've just got time for a shower.

Garrard exits into the bedroom, taking his bag with him

Prosser Run after him, Tom.
Olley Be quite a funny scene. (*To Mrs Rogers*) Told us, my love, didn't you.
Prosser I bet she hasn't locked the door, either.

They wait

Hewlett I thought he was in Manchester today?
Prosser I shan't be happy until he's had a good fiddle with that display.

Garrard enters, thoughtful

Olley Sorry, John. Entirely my fault. But you did say you were coming tomorrow. I shouldn't have taken any notice of that.
Garrard That display—there's a market there, you know. You look at those stands they've got down there in the exhibition. Ten thousand pounds each, three goes out of them, and they're finished. We could offer them a permanent unit. Standard Modus components. Make it up into any shape they liked. What do you think?
Olley We could get the drawing office to sketch something out. John . . .

Anni enters, wrapped in a towel, amused

Anni I'm so sorry! I should have locked the door!
Olley This is Miss Friedrich.
Prosser It was our little surprise for you, Mr Garrard.
Anni No, but it was funny! I feel this cold air on my back and I'm completely naked, and I turn round, and here is this man, he stands and he looks at the floor and he thinks!
Garrard The selling points would be: a quality timber finish instead of hardboard; a fresh layout for each exhibition; and

price. If we could market it for, what, twenty thousand ...
What do you think?

Olley John, Miss Friedrich is manning our stand down in the hall.

Garrard I thought you were meeting your boy-friend at six?

Anni Oh!

Olley What? What?

Anni It's him!

Olley You've met already?

Anni How much rent do I pay? Who do I live with?

Olley Oh, I see. This is the bloke. I might have guessed. Well, let me introduce him. Mr Garrard. Our Managing Director.

Anni Oh, *no!* (*She covers her face in embarrassment*)

Olley (*amused*) Sent him off with a flea in his ear, did you?

Anni I think I was a little bit rude.

Olley Don't worry. I don't suppose he noticed. He's always asking questions, but then by the time you give him the answer he's started worrying about something else. Isn't that right, John?

Garrard Uh-huh, uh-huh. Anyway, let's get a price on it. We can't do anything till we've got a price. Colin, I've got a job for you.

Hewlett Yes, Mr Garrard?

Olley (*to Anni*) You see?

Garrard (*to Olley*) What?

Olley All right, John, we'll get a price out.

Garrard (*to Hewlett*) Go downstairs. Go into the restaurant. (*To Olley*) I can think what happens next and still hear all I need to hear Tom, don't you worry. (*To Hewlett*) Restaurant—bars—all the public rooms. (*To Anni*) Not going to stand there all night in nothing but a wet bath-towel, are you? (*To Olley*) Because if I wanted to sit on my backside and brood about the past I wouldn't be making building components—I'd be digging up flint axes. (*To Anni*) Name and firm—everyone who comes to the stand—no matter what they ask you—ask you to marry them, makes no difference—just get their name and the name of their firm.

Anni exits into the bedroom

(*To Hewlett*) Right through the hotel. Get up on a chair. Know what Parker Matthews fill their doors with?

Hewlett Yes.
Garrard Tell me whose doors they all are.
Hewlett Right.

Hewlett exits

Prosser Nice girl, though. Real plus on the stand.
Garrard Workers' rights.
Olley Oh. Believes in them, does she?
Garrard Organizes all the guest-workers in the big hotels. Turks.
    Greeks. All her spare time. She and her boy-friend. Tells them
    their legal rights. Stirs them up.

Pause

Olley Ted Shaw was right, then.
Prosser (*to Garrard*) Not throwing bombs, is she?
Olley Wants to smash it all up one way or another. Those were
    bombs going off, you know, John.
Prosser Not worried, are you, Mr Garrard?
Garrard (*brooding*) Go to the station, wouldn't you.

Olley and Prosser exchange looks

    Go on a Sunday. That's where you'd start. Ever noticed a
    German railway station on a Sunday? Full of foreign guest-
    workers. Standing around and talking—nowhere else to go . . .
Prosser Not careful, he'll be out there helping her.
Garrard So what are we going to talk to this Hungarian about?
Prosser Walls, I assume.
Garrard No, for a start. Chat, chat, chat. Kids—he'll have kids.
    Got any snapshots on you, Frank?
Olley John, don't start planning the conversation in advance.
Garrard We could all be sitting here in silence for ten minutes.
Olley Just let it happen, John. God will provide.
Garrard That's a point. Hungarian. Be a Catholic, won't he.
Olley What about it?
Garrard Give you something to go on.
Olley What, tell our rosaries together? Little chat about the lives
    of the saints?
Garrard Tom, you've gone around being a Catholic all these
    years like a bed with brass knobs on, and I've never been able
    to see what use it was.

Olley (*good-humouredly*) I'll tell you what the use of my religion is, John. It's to keep you out of jail. We've got to have one man on the Board with some kind of morals or we'd have ceased trading years ago.

Anni enters from the bedroom, dressed

Garrard (*looking at his watch*) Three minutes. What are we going to do for three minutes?

Prosser indicates Garrard's shoes to Anni

Anni What?

Prosser puts his finger to his lips

Garrard What? What?
Anni (*realizing*) Oh . . .
Garrard What? What? What?
Anni (*to Prosser*) I can't! It's impossible! Not now!
Garrard What? What? What? What? Can't what? What's impossible?
Anni (*laughing*) Scheisse . . .! (*She covers her face again*)
Olley Me again, I'm afraid, John. I made a bet she couldn't get your shoes off.
Prosser She took ours off, you see.
Anni Oh, it's worse each moment!
Olley We were just fooling around.
Prosser Anyway, I've lost, I've lost.
Garrard Be late, won't he. Standing here half the night. Might as well have a shower. (*He moves towards the bedroom*)
Anni Wait, wait! (*With the most winning disarming candour*) If Mr Prosser wins, I get half the money. So please, just be very kind and sit down and I'll take your shoes off. (*She smiles irresistibly at him, and takes his arm*)
Garrard (*to Prosser*) How much are you losing?
Prosser Ten pounds.

Garrard gives a small, brief laugh, then exits into the bedroom

Olley Made him laugh, anyway.
Prosser The bastard.
Anni He doesn't like women, perhaps?
Prosser No idea. Can you make walls out of them?

Olley (*diplomatically*) Mystery to me, that man.

Anni A mystery? Oh, but that's good when someone is a mystery!

Olley Bit of a mystery yourself, aren't you?

Anni Yes?

Olley Organizing Turks.

Anni Oh.

Olley We didn't know about that, did we.

Prosser (*to Olley, getting his wallet out*) Pounds—or do you want it in marks?

Garrard enters

Garrard If he turns up while I'm in the shower . . .

Prosser Don't worry, Mr Garrard. We'll get started on the family snaps.

Garrard thinks

Garrard Right.

Garrard exits

Prosser Thought he'd changed his mind.

Olley Hadn't even got his tie off. What's he doing out there?

Prosser (*throwing down the money*) Don't spend it all on drink, then.

Anni (*intercepting the money and giving it back to Prosser*) Wait, wait. There still may be chances to win.

Prosser No, he'll be off back to London first thing in the morning, won't he, Tom?

Anni So, it's not the morning yet. Who knows what will happen to people's shoes.

Anni exits

Mrs Rogers goes to the door

Prosser Got her eye on him, hasn't she.

Olley I think John had better keep his door locked tonight.

A click as Mrs Rogers slips the catch. Prosser and Olley look round

Prosser Oh. There's service.

Mrs Rogers It's his room now. He doesn't want people strolling in.

Prosser She certainly looks after him, your Mrs R.

Mrs Rogers Fancy putting her up to that!

Prosser What, the shoes?

Mrs Rogers You make a fool of him.

Olley Oh, come on! We were the ones with egg on our faces. *He* just laughed!

Mrs Rogers You all play up to him.

Olley *We* play up to *him*? *He* plays up to *us*! Walking in like that—shouting for a chair—inspecting the door!

Mrs Rogers Yes, because he knows he's going to get a reaction.

Olley He doesn't look to see whether he's getting a reaction or not.

Mrs Rogers He doesn't need to. He knows you all lap it up.

Olley He knows we're all going to be talking about him as soon as he's out of the room.

Mrs Rogers Yes, and one day he'll come walking right back in and . . .

A crash, and the main door reverberates heavily in its frame. They turn guiltily, Prosser crosses and opens the door

> *Hewlett enters, tenderly cupping his nose. He takes his hand away, and inspects it for blood*

Hewlett I thought we kept it on the latch?

Prosser Trying to keep surprises out. (*He looks at Mrs Rogers*) Unless we're trying to keep surprises in.

Mrs Rogers ignores this, and returns to her desk

> Hidden fires there, Tom.

Olley All right, Frank, give it a rest.

Hewlett Anyway, they're German.

Prosser Who?

Hewlett The doors.

Prosser Oh, that was quick.

Hewlett The manager told me.

Olley The manager—shrewd move.

Hewlett No, the barman called him. I was standing on a barstool. Is he always like this?

Prosser Garrard? Oh, he's only just warming up. Isn't he, Tom?

Olley No, he'll settle down in a minute.

Prosser His brain's got all shaken up in transit.

Olley Once he's had his shower, done a bit of business, eaten a meal, he'll be quite human.

Prosser (*anxiously*) He'll eat with you and Goetz, will he?

Olley Unless you're volunteering?

Prosser How about Colin?

Olley Bit of a plateful for a youngster.

Prosser Perhaps this Hungarian bloke will have the honour.

Olley He certainly won't eat on his own.

Prosser Met a Hungarian! Oh, bloody hell.

Olley Trust John.

Prosser Met a Hungarian in a taxi! God bless us all.

Olley Where did he find you? (*To Hewlett*) You know where he hired Frank? In the waiting-room at Golders Green Crematorium.

Prosser Ted Shaw's old pal—Pat McGuire—it was his funeral. They were running ten minutes late.

Olley So naturally, John wondered how to fill in the time . . .

Garrard enters

Prosser He's back.

Olley John, you can't have showered in that time.

Garrard What do you think, Tom—Ian Weatherall?

Olley What about him?

Garrard To run Manchester. When Sydney Laver goes.

Olley Sidney's not retiring for another two years yet.

Garrard No, I was just thinking.

Olley All you've been doing, standing out there thinking?

Garrard (*sitting*) I want a big effort with this Hungarian. That's where the markets are—Eastern Europe. That's where they're building. Planned economy—no slumps. Centralized purchasing—big orders, big runs. That's where we want to be . . . No sign?

Olley Not yet. Colin found out about those doors for you, though. They're all German.

Garrard Uh-huh, uh-huh . . . (*He thinks*)

Prosser And Mrs Rogers has been tidying up the stand. Emptied all the ashtrays. Got everything nice, look.

Garrard Uh-huh, uh-huh.

Olley She could go, couldn't she, John?

Mrs Rogers I think I'd better stay on for a little while, thank you, Mr Olley, just in case I'm needed.

Olley (*to Garrard*) She's had a pretty long day.

Prosser Working away on the stand. Have you noticed, Mr Garrard?

Garrard Uh-huh . . . What do Essex want, then, Frank?

Prosser Essex?

Garrard Thought your boy had his interview this week?

Prosser Oh, *Essex*. Two Bs and a C.

Garrard Two Bs? And Warwick wanted one? What did Sheffield want? Sheffield wanted one. So, what, Essex are good, are they?

Prosser I suppose they must be.

Olley (*to Hewlett*) Close personal interest in his staff, you see. Famous for it.

Garrard (*to Olley*) Hasn't got anything else to do, has she?

Mrs Rogers No.

Garrard Nothing to do, nowhere to go. Might as well stay and work like the rest of us. (*To Prosser*) Then what? After he's finished university?

Prosser I don't know.

Garrard Come into the firm. What, three years, four years time? We'll be in Europe. Could be in Eastern Europe. Polish, Frank, get him learning Polish.

Prosser Polish. I'll tell him.

Garrard What, you mean he wouldn't join the firm?

Prosser You know what kids are like.

Olley Turn their noses up at industry.

Prosser Not only kids. The whole world looks down on us.

Olley Funny, when you think about it. Because we're the ones who put the whole world *up!* You'd think we'd get some credit for that.

Garrard Where is he, then?

Prosser What, now? At school.

Garrard No, this Hungarian. What's his name? (*He gets the card out of his pocket*) Horvath.

Olley Shared a taxi with someone else.

Garrard (*to Prosser*) Snaps? Got the snaps, have you?

Prosser Perhaps Colin's got some.

Hewlett What?

Prosser Mr Garrard wants someone to show this Hungarian
their family snaps. Break the ice. All human beings together.
Hewlett (*getting his wallet out*) It's just the kids.
Prosser I knew Colin'd have some.
Hewlett Is this the sort of thing?

*Hewlett hands the stack of snaps to Garrard, who looks slowly
through them, absorbed*

That's Mark, my older boy. He's four. It's not a very good one
of him, actually, he's much more—That's him before he had
his hair cut. He looks terrible there—Oh, well, I got the sun in
the lens. I just left it in because it gives you an idea what the
garden—That's Jonathan. Nineteen months. No, just a
moment, where are we? *Twenty* months. Well, he was fifteen
months when that picture was taken. No, sorry, let's see, that
was *before* Whitsun . . .
Garrard (*to Olley*) I don't know what you mean, "personal
interest".
Olley Personal interest? Where are we now?
Garrard Of course I take a personal interest.
Olley In the staff? Of course you do, John. Of course. Of course.
of course.

*Garrard returns to the snaps and gazes at the one he was looking at
before*

Hewlett (*after a respectful interval*) Fourteen months.
Garrard What?
Hewlett Sorry. Jonathan. In that picture.

Garrard gazes at it, then looks up at Olley

Garrard Got to keep the buggers happy.
Olley Of course. So what do you think of Colin's snaps, then,
John?

Garrard studies them again, and turns over another picture

Hewlett That's Mark and Jonathan together, only Jonathan
moved.
Garrard (*handing the snaps back to Hewlett*) Colin . . .
Hewlett Yes?

Garrard Go downstairs and look in the foyer. He may be waiting down there.

Hewlett Oh, right. But how will I . . . ?

Garrard About my height. No, smaller, smaller. Grey suit. Hungarian accent.

Hewlett Oh. Well. Yes. Right.

Olley John . . .

Garrard What?

Olley Say something.

Garrard What do you mean?

Olley About his snaps.

Garrard (*to Hewlett*) Polaroid, aren't they?

Hewlett Yes, Polaroid. Thank you. Well . . .

Hewlett exits

Garrard Give him something to do, anyway. Take his mind off his troubles.

Prosser Troubles? What troubles does *he* have? He's just a kid.

Garrard He's homesick.

Prosser Homesick?

Olley Haven't you noticed?

Garrard Sitting there with an egg in his throat.

Prosser But he's a grown man!

Garrard On the road all week at home?

Prosser Gets back to Bristol most nights.

Garrard That's the time, though, isn't it? Kids shouting "Daddy! Daddy! Daddy!" when you come in. Wife still in bikinis.

Prosser You never felt homesick, did you, Mr Garrard?

Olley Oh, we'd been in the war. Anyway, we were too busy. Weren't we, John?

Garrard (*seeing a set of records*) What have you been buying yourself this time, Frank? More Wagner?

Prosser Not this time. You always wanted to get home to the kids, though, did you, Mr Garrard? I can't imagine you as a family man. But you were, were you?

Garrard Beethoven. You've got these already.

Prosser I've got the Klemperer and the Karajan. This is the Kubelik.

Garrard Better, is he, this bloke?

Prosser Different.

Garrard (*reading the record box*) Know a lot about Beethoven, do you, Frank?

Olley Frank knows everything about music. No—he does! All the keys, all the opus numbers. Ask him some questions. (*He looks over Garrard's shoulder*) E flat major. Which one's that?

Prosser The Eroica.

Olley What's the Eighth?

Prosser F major.

Olley Opus . . .?

Prosser Ninety-three.

Olley What about the fourth?

Prosser B flat major. Opus sixty.

Olley You see? Ask him about wine. He can tell you all the châteaus, all the good years.

Garrard (*brooding*) What's the difference between E flat major and B flat major?

Prosser What do you mean, what's the difference?

Garrard Why did he do one in one and the other in the other?

Prosser Well, I think different keys are associated with different moods, aren't they?

Garrard What's the mood that goes with B flat major?

Prosser I don't know.

Garrard Know which is which when you hear them, do you?

Prosser What, me? Or Beethoven?

Garrard You.

Prosser No.

Silence

Olley We've lost him.

Prosser I don't think I've passed.

Olley (*to Garrard*) Ask him which are the good years for Beaujolais.

Garrard gets up and crosses to the window

Now where's he off to?

Prosser Admiring the view.

Garrard Pack it down a manhole, wouldn't you?

Pause. Olley and Prosser exchange looks

Olley Pack it down a manhole? Pack what down a manhole?

Pause. Garrard continues to gaze out of the window

Prosser (*to Olley*) Could be the Beaujolais.

Olley (*to Prosser*) Could be the Beethoven.

Garrard Explosive. Just pick the right manhole and you'd get the lot. Gas, water. Electricity, telephones. Sewage. Whole block out of action. Whole street full of shit.

Prosser (*amused*) Build it up—blow it up. It's all the same to Mr Garrard.

Garrard Just thinking how you'd make it work.

Olley Do it, too, if you got the chance, wouldn't you, John?

Garrard Wouldn't you?

Olley Me? I'd smack their silly bottoms for them.

Garrard Anyone smack yours?

Olley What do you mean?

Garrard Doing the same thing at their age, weren't you?

Olley Me?

Garrard Flattened the whole city.

Olley Oh, I see . . . Well, we never did Frankfurt.

Garrard You did Hamburg.

Olley Yes, we did Hamburg. And Cologne. And Kassel. And Essen and Dortmund and Duisburg.

Prosser Wasn't you personally, was it, Tom? You were just the navigator, weren't you? Got them there, got them home.

Garrard Typical bloody Tom.

Olley It looked like the end of the world down there some nights. I thought that was that.

Prosser Incredible, really, isn't it? There's Hamburg now— there's Frankfurt, there's Dortmund—as thick on the ground as ever.

Olley Like woodland. Burn it back, and up it comes green next season. Like our walls—it's all demountable. As long as people have still got the ideas in their heads. As long as they've got the skills in their hands.

Prosser So you'll be wasting your time with those bombs, Mr Garrard.

Garrard (*still looking out of the window*) I'll tell you why he did it, though.

Prosser and Olley mock him behind his back

Olley What are we on to now, John?

Garrard I'll tell you why he wrote one in E flat major and one in B flat major.

Olley You're not still worrying about that?

Garrard No, I'll tell you. It's because there he was with the pen in his hand and the paper in front of him, and there was E flat major. And when he'd done E flat major, there was B flat major.

Prosser Maybe. Maybe.

Garrard But where do you come in?

Prosser Where do *I* come in?

Garrard You're listening to this symphony, you've got your eyes closed—you're doing something inside your head. What is it?

Prosser I don't think I'm doing anything. I think I'm just listening. Aren't I?

Garrard You mean you're thinking, this is where it goes up and this is where it goes down and this is the bit where it goes like this and this is the bit where it goes like this other bit?

Olley No, he's just sitting there enjoying it. Aren't you, Frank?

Garrard What do you know about music?

Olley I don't know anything about music, but I know how to sit still and enjoy something. Unlike some people.

Garrard (*sitting*) I'll sit still and enjoy myself when we've got some orders in the book. Just find out if this Hungarian's going to give us something, then I'll sit back and look at my toes. (*Pause*) True, though, Frank. Know what I want to do when I retire? I'll tell you: nothing. Sit around in my braces. No shaving, eat out of tins. Lie back in the chair all day, watch the flies walk round the ceiling. (*Pause*) I'll tell you what I want to do. I want to get this firm into Eastern Europe. Frank, go and look downstairs. Colin's probably wandering round like a lost sheep himself.

A knock

Ah.

Olley Patience rewarded.

Garrard Frank, you let him in . . . Hold on, hold on . . . Tom . . .

Olley stands

Sit down, sit down. Now, don't rush him. Friendly drinks, that's all. I'll stand here . . . I'll sit . . . I'll stand . . . Come on,

then, Frank, open the bloody door. He'll have gone back to
Hungary by now.

Prosser opens the door

Shaw enters

Shaw Is he here?
Garrard Oh, it's you, is it?
Shaw He is, too. What a surprise.

They shake hands

Garrard What do you want, then?
Shaw Just thought I might get a nice little surprise if I popped my
    head in now.
Olley He gave us all a surprise. Didn't he, Frank?
Shaw I saw your Mr Hewlett downstairs. Playing some game of
    detectives in the lobby. And I thought, would Tom Olley have
    kept a man on the hop all evening like that when he should be
    out enjoying himself? And I thought, Never! Not Tom Olley!
    And I thought, who do I know who'd do a thing like that?
Garrard Good of you to look in, Ted. But . . .
Shaw Only a small one, then, John, only a small one.
Garrard Can't give you a drink now, Ted.
Shaw Trying to keep the bill down are you, John?
Garrard Busy, busy.
Shaw (*to Olley*) Never stops, does he? Like a hamster let out of
    its cage. This way, nibble nibble. That way, nibble, nibble.
    Take your eyes off him for a minute and you've a hole in the
    carpet.
Garrard I've got a meeting.
Shaw Worst thing is when he stops still for a moment with one
    paw in the air and just looks at you. What's he thinking about
    behind those beady little nibbling eyes? Is it the carpet? Or is
    it the sofa? Or is it you?
Garrard See you on the stand tomorrow, then, Ted.
Shaw Something's going to get nibbled, though. You can rely
    on that. Something's going to get chewed up and turned into
    a hamster's nest. So you're expecting someone, are you, John?
Garrard Should have been here ten minutes ago.

Shaw A little tip, then, John. If you want to get in his good
  books, talk to him about spaniels ... You didn't know, did
  you? His wife breeds them.

Olley (*to Garrard*) Peter Davis.

Garrard Peter Davis?

Shaw I knew him in the old days, you see. When he was just
  starting up in sixty-eight with Portobello Investments.

Olley Mr Shaw thinks you're over here to meet him.

Garrard He's in Brussels. They told me he was in Brussels. So
  what—he's not in Brussels?

Shaw He's in Frankfurt.

Garrard And what—you've seen him?

Shaw Hasn't been near me.

Prosser I thought he was in New York all this week.

Garrard Brussels, Brussels. I was talking to his secretary this
  morning.

Shaw So it's not me and it's not you.

Pause

Garrard Could be anybody.

Shaw He could be here for his summer holidays.

Pause

Prosser I'll tell you someone who's here. Talbot.

Shaw Ronnie Talbot?

Olley British Paper Group?

Prosser Saw him at the opera last night.

Pause

Shaw Davis wouldn't do that. Would he, John? He wouldn't sell
  me to British Paper?

Garrard Restructure the Group one way or another. What
  they've brought him in for.

Shaw You'd do it, wouldn't you? You'd sell off a company like
  so many square feet of walling.

Garrard I don't see what the worry is. Your firm'd fit into
  British Paper all right.

Shaw *I* shouldn't.

Garrard No, you'd get a handshake.

Shaw John, that company's my life!

Garrard (*embarrassed and impatient*) Oh, come on, come on, come on. Not going to burst into tears over a bit of business.

Shaw (*to Olley*) I've embarrassed him now, look. But it's a hard crust to choke down, isn't it? Everybody talks about John here. Everybody knows how *he* does it. Lives it and breathes it from the moment he gets up to the moment he goes to bed. But what about me? Do you think I don't arrive as early and stay as late? Do you think I don't bend as low over the work? But in the end he's justified by it and I'm not. Look at him, though. I've put him right off his supper, haven't I?

Garrard Ted, this meeting . . .

Shaw Don't worry, John. I won't embarrass you further. You get those little teeth of yours into the woodwork. Bye-bye, Frank. Bye-bye, Tom.

Prosser Good-bye, Mr Shaw.

Olley And don't worry about it. We're all in the dark. We don't know what he's up to.

Shaw No—maybe he'll sell John here instead. Get a better price for him.

Shaw exits

Prosser I'll never get my toes straight again.

Olley Poor Ted.

Prosser Like a slug, isn't he? Fat and full of himself. Then you tread on him, and—*squirt!*

Olley No, but he's right—he worries away just as much as bloody John. They're both crippled by their trade. Like a couple of old miners with the dust. Nothing in their chests but stone. Isn't that right, John?

Garrard What do you think, then?

Olley What, about Ted?

Garrard Davis, Davis.

Olley Well, I suppose, yes, Peter Davis might well be trying to get rid of Securex.

Garrard No, us. Is he selling *us?*

Prosser What? That was just Ted Shaw whistling in the dark.

Olley (*thinking*) Get cash for us, couldn't he?

Garrard Get cash and pump it into Ted.

Prosser You're joking!

Olley Stranger things have happened in this business.

Prosser Well, I suppose Talbot would be quite pleased to have a good solid moneyspinner as part of British Paper.

Olley Don't be silly, Frank. He'd close us down. Clear the market for their J. C. Wickham and Sons.

Prosser Oh.

Olley Well, don't worry about it, John. You'd be looked after.

Garrard You wouldn't.

Olley Watch the flies on the ceiling.

Pause

Prosser (*touching the walls in the display*) We might be selling nothing.

Olley (*to Garrard*) And you really didn't know Peter Davis was in Frankfurt today?

Garrard No. Thought it was tomorrow.

Olley Ah. Ah.

Prosser What? I don't understand. You *are* meeting him here?

Olley *That's* why John's come today. Get in a day ahead of him.

Prosser I suppose that's why Peter Davis is here today, is it? To get in a day ahead of Mr Garrard?

They both look at Garrard. Garrard broods

Olley If you're meeting him tomorrow, John, he's not selling you today.

Garrard No, I was thinking about Frank.

Prosser Me?

Garrard You might be just the man for the job.

Olley Which job is this?

Garrard Opening up in Eastern Europe.

Olley John, we haven't even shown one Hungarian the samples yet!

Garrard (*to Prosser*) No, you want to get away from your wife, don't you?

Olley Oh, John, for heaven's sake!

Garrard What? Not a secret, is it?

Olley John, let me explain. This is a human being, not a consignment of chipboard.

Prosser It's all right. It doesn't worry me.

Garrard *He* doesn't mind. Don't give me a lecture on how to handle people, Tom. No use tiptoeing round like an undertaker.

Man's got two heads—he's got two heads. Can't just talk to one and shut your eyes every time the other one looks round at you.

Olley I know what *you'd* do, if you met a man with two heads. You'd ask him if he had to pay full price for both haircuts. Anyway, Frank hasn't got two heads.

Garrard No, he's got two women! What? Frank's not embarrassed.

Olley looks at Mrs Rogers

Garrard Is she still here? I thought she'd gone home. She knows all this. You're the one who's playing auntie, as usual. (*To Prosser*) So what do you think, then, Frank? Give you another couple of thousand. More expenses to fiddle. Two women? You could have women in every country from the Black Sea to the Baltic.

Prosser Well . . .

Olley (*tactfully*) I suggest we at any rate talk to this Hungarian gentleman before we ask Frank to cancel the milk at home.

Garrard (*looking at his watch*) Yes, where is he? Frank, go down and see what Colin's up to.

Olley Not coming, your bloke, is he. You know what these East Europeans are like.

Garrard Frank . . . (*To Olley*) Better than sitting here putting up with me.

Prosser I'll give Colin a hand. Three heads are better than one.

Prosser exits

Olley He's probably been arrested for talking to you.

Garrard moves restlessly to the window and looks out

I'd go and have that shower.

Garrard If we're not going to be in Eastern Europe then we've got to be in here somewhere.

Olley I don't know how you can go on gazing at this bloody town, John.

Garrard Thought you liked it.

Olley Me?

Garrard Stop them blowing it up.

Olley (*thinking*) The only thing I like in this town is the river.

Garrard Pretty, is it?

Olley Pretty? (*He thinks*) No, it's not pretty. It's not anything much. I think that's what I like about it. It's not square, it's not circular. It's not dear, it's not cheap. You can't wipe it down with a damp cloth. It can't be turned round or taken to pieces or resited to suit changing office needs. It's just a great lump of water, falling slowly downhill forever.

Pause

Garrard German, are they?

Olley What?

Garrard The doors downstairs.

Olley John . . .

Garrard What?

Olley Just—*stop*.

Garrard (*looking at his watch*) I'll have a shower, then. Fire-resistant, though, isn't it.

Olley The shower?

Garrard The river. Fire-resistant and flexible and cheap. You just give me that river Tom—I'll make something out of it.

Garrard exits into the bedroom, then returns

German?

Olley Yes.

Garrard exits

He'll kill himself in the end, though. The doctor's told him, I've told him. But he only hears what he wants to hear. He doesn't smoke, he doesn't drink, so he thinks he's safe.

Mrs Rogers You make him worse, though, don't you. The worse he behaves, the better you like it.

Olley Not me! I'm always taking the matches out of his hands. I'm always putting the carving-knife out of his reach.

Mrs Rogers So he knows you're not going to let him go too far. You make him behave like a spoilt child.

Olley My sweet precious, he's the same with everyone! He's driven his wife into a home—his daughter's in Canada, never writes—his son no-one knows where he is—on a building-site when last heard of. This is his life! And it'll be the death of him. (*Pause*) At least he knows what he wants. That's his great strength. That's why he's got us all dancing through the streets behind him.

Mrs Rogers Knows what he wants! That's just what he doesn't know! He's lost. He's like a little lost child. All he wants is . . .

Garrard enters, holding a little magazine

Garrard How long did this one take you, then?

Olley Where did you find that?

Garrard In the bathroom.

Olley Oh, I wrote it one lunch-hour.

Garrard (*reading*) "Through all the year's accumulated gold I flounder
                          In sun-shot beechen glooms
                          Like gilded drawing-rooms;
                          And my sad heart again fills as of old
                          With golden wonder."

Mrs Rogers Excuse me.

Mrs Rogers exits

Garrard "Flounder"—"wonder"—that's all right, that's a rhyme, is it?

Olley Yes.

Garrard Who says whether it's all right or not?

Olley I think I do, don't I?

Garrard Very nice, anyway, Tom. How much this time?

Olley I don't know—a tenner. She has, though, hasn't she—she's got a bit of a thing about you. Frank's right.

Garrard Who? What?

Olley Mrs R. Had it for years, when you come to think about it. Sad, isn't it, sometimes, life?

Garrard A tenner—that's not bad. And you'll soon have enough for a book. What—thirty poems? Thirty poems at a tenner each. So it'll cost you what, about three hundred quid? Cheaper than keeping a woman on the side, anyway. (*Pause*) Why, did she say something?

Olley Funny, really. I picked her for the trip to play safe. Wouldn't have any husbands making fools of themselves. Wouldn't have any wives losing sleep at home. Never thought about it the other way round, what she might be feeling.

Garrard What did she say?
Olley Nothing. Suddenly dawned on me.

Hewlett enters

Hewlett Sorry. Frank's taken over. He told me to come back and
sit down for a bit.
Olley He's not coming now, John. You'd better eat with me and
Goetz. I'll run down and tell Frank he can knock off, shall I?
Hewlett I'll go.
Olley Sit down, sit down. All right, John?
Garrard Uh-huh. And what—forty, forty-one?

Pause. Olley looks at Garrard

Older? Younger?
Olley John, you're not getting any ideas, are you?
Garrard What's all this, Tom?
Olley She's had a difficult life. I know I go on at her. The last
thing she needs is any complications.
Garrard Tom, I only asked how old she was!
Olley All right, John. I know. Of course you wouldn't. But I'm
serious about this. You know I'm serious about things some-
times.
Garrard Yes, yes.
Olley Anyway, I don't know how old she is, because I've never
asked her. And you still haven't had that shower, have you?

Olley exits

Garrard stands lost in thought. Hewlett does not like to sit down

Hewlett It was funny. Tom and Frank said the first thing you'd
do when you arrived was you'd rearrange the display.

No response

We all stood here watching you. Every time you went towards
the display we held our breath.

No response

It was funny.
Garrard Two boys?
Hewlett Yes.

Garrard So now your house is too small.

Hewlett It's a flat. We're building an extra room. Well, I'm dividing one of the rooms into two.

Garrard Using the product?

Hewlett (*laughing*) I can't afford it.

Garrard (*sharply*) What do you mean, you can't afford it?

Hewlett Well, it's only cheaper if you're saving labour costs. I haven't got any to save, because it's my labour.

Garrard What, you're not stealing the samples? I thought all the reps built their houses out of samples.

Hewlett No, I'm a Christian.

Garrard Oh yes. Tom was telling me. Sudden was it?

Mrs Rogers enters

Hewlett It took the best part of a year. Because I struggled against it. I didn't want to give in. But in the end the Lord Jesus simply came and took hold of me.

Mrs Rogers I'm sorry. (*She goes to her desk*)

Garrard Took hold of you? What does that mean?

Hewlett I mean literally took hold of me! Or that's what it felt like. I got this terrible stiffness in the neck, as if something was trying to bend it and I was trying to keep it straight. I know it sounds funny—I thought I was going mad. In the end I couldn't hold out any longer. I bent my neck and surrendered.

Garrard That was before the kids were born?

Hewlett Before I was married.

Garrard And what, it made you happier?

Hewlett It transformed me. Because I'm not just my own empty self any more—I'm filled with Christ. And the things around me are not just empty things. They're filled, carrying a kind of electric charge, because they're all part of the dominion of Christ Jesus.

Garrard (*looking at Mrs Rogers*) Uh-huh. Uh-huh.

Hewlett (*taking a booklet from his pocket*) I've a little book here which you might just possibly find of interest.

Garrard (*taking it*) So you're off to dinner now, are you?

Hewlett Oh, right. Thank you. (*He hesitates*) I hope it didn't embarrass you. I mean, it doesn't embarrass me, talking about it, but I know it embarrasses some people. Well, then . . . (*He retires towards the door, embarrassed*)

Garrard Colin . . .

Hewlett stops

> When you get to your room, pick up the phone and give your
> wife a ring. Set her mind at rest.

Hewlett Well, we're trying to save money . . .

Garrard On the bill, Colin, on the bill.

Hewlett Oh, well, thank you. Thank you, Mr Garrard.

Garrard Oh, and Colin . . .

Hewlett Yes, Mr Garrard?

Garrard What *have* you got in the wall, then?

Hewlett You mean—Christ?

Garrard No . . .

Hewlett Oh—breeze blocks.

Garrard Ah.

Hewlett exits

Mrs Rogers I'm sorry. I didn't realize you were having a private
conversation.

Garrard (*flatly*) Like to eat?

Mrs Rogers I beg your pardon?

Garrard Eat, eat. Want to eat?

Mrs Rogers You mean—with you and Mr Olley?

Garrard Tom? No, Tom's taking this German fellow out.

Mrs Rogers (*reaching for the telephone*) You want me to order
some sandwiches?

Garrard Dinner, dinner.

Mrs Rogers You mean—in a restaurant?

Garrard What?

Mrs Rogers You're—inviting me out to dinner?

Garrard Dinner—yes. Food. Eat.

Mrs Rogers Well, it's very . . . I'm not sure I really . . . I mean,
it really is very . . . I'll go and change.

Olley enters

Olley Frank's gone off to pick up Verhaeren. They've got ice-
skating on the telly tonight, Mrs R, so you'll be all right. (*To
Garrard*) Now we're meeting Mr Goetz in the bar downstairs
at eight o'clock . . .

Garrard Count me out.

Olley Oh. I thought you said . . . ?
Garrard Change of plan.

Olley stares at Garrard. Then he looks at Mrs Rogers

Mrs Rogers Excuse me.

   Mrs Rogers exits

Olley Another engagement?
Garrard What? What? What's all this?
Olley A dinner engagement?
Garrard Look, just tell me—are we seeing Verhaeren in the
  morning? What have you fixed?

   *Mrs Rogers enters, followed by Dr Horvath. He is a middle-aged
   man, all smiles and charm, and he is carrying a mass of shopping*

Olley does not see them

Olley I could bite my tongue out. Can't resist it, can you? All
  anyone's got to say to you is, "John, there's one thing I really
  beg of you not to do" and as soon as their back's turned that's
  the very thing you immediately go and do . . . !

But Garrard has already crossed to shake Horvath's hand

Garrard Dr Horvath . . .
Horvath Oh! Mr Garrard! I am so sorry!

   Mrs Rogers exits

  I must buy so many things! My wife, my sister-in-law, my
  children—they all say, oh, you're going to West Germany?
  Then you must bring me back Levis, you must bring me back
  clothes for the baby, you must bring me back books and
  sausages and some special scissors for cutting hair and some
  special little smart jacket for the dog, and I don't know, I don't
  know!
Garrard Right, then. Drink, drink. What do you want to drink?
Olley (*tactfully*) Shall we just put some of that stuff out of the
  way first?
Horvath (*gratefully*) Oh! You're so kind!
Garrard This is Tom Olley, my Sales Director.

Horvath I am so pleased to meet you!

Horvath and Olley dispose of the shopping. Garrard waits by the drinks

I had to run here, I had to run there. And everywhere—so many things! My eyes were jumping this way, that way. It's fantastic. But you know what they say in Germany?—*Wahl ist Qual*—choosing is painful.

Garrard Whisky? Gin? Vodka?

Horvath Oh! How charming! No thank you. You come to Budapest, Mr Garrard. What would your wife ask you to buy in Budapest?

Garrard So you've got children, have you? What, boys—girls? How old are they?

Horvath Two girls. And these are your walls. (*He inspects the display*)

Garrard Two girls? (*To Olley*) Where's Colin? Hasn't taken his bloody snaps away with him, has he? (*To Horvath*) Anyway, Tom here's got girls. Three girls, haven't you, Tom. Pictures— got any pictures of them?

Olley (*taking out his wallet*) Well, they're grown up now. Got children of their own.

Garrard They'll do. Come on.

Horvath (*feeling the wall units*) Oh! Oh! But this is beautiful! The standard of work is so high! I feel this surface and it's like putting my hand on silk. You know what I wish? I wish my brother-in-law could see this. Because Ferenc—he has a good appreciation of these things, he'd be so happy.

Olley (*offering a photograph*) These are my eldest daughter's two, on the beach in Brittany.

Garrard (*pushing the photographs back*) Yes, well, the point is, it's a complete system.

Horvath Wonderful, wonderful.

Garrard The only system with uniform finishes for the load-bearing and demountable elements.

Horvath Unique system.

Garrard You can't see where one stops and the next one starts until I unlock the panel, so, and . . .

Horvath And they move. But this is perfect.

Garrard This *is* what you're looking for?

Horvath Perfect. No, really and truly, I congratulate you. You are masters of your trade.

Garrard looks at Olley, disconcerted

Olley (*anxiously*) We offer them in a range of core materials.

Horvath (*working the units*) Of course.

Olley Extruded chipboard, where weight is a factor. Inert European flaxboard . . .

Horvath Wonderful, wonderful.

Olley That's for thirty-minute fire resistance. Then for sixty-minute fire-resistance . . .

Horvath And these surfaces look so elegant, so rich.

Olley Well, as far as surfaces go, we can offer, ex-stock, a choice of abura, afrormosia, agba, bird's eye maple . . .

Horvath Wonderful. And it's a twelve hundred millimetre module?

Olley Twelve hundred mil, yes. Or Columbian pine, Honduras mahogany . . .

Horvath Oh, but this is the answer to our prayers. You do these things so well in England. The engineering intelligence is so original. Your commercial approach is so clever.

Olley Oh. Well . . . Very kind . . .

Garrard Right, then, let's get down to it.

Horvath Prices.

Olley Prices. Right. (*He fetches a list from the desk*)

Horvath We must just talk a little about prices.

Olley This is our current price-list.

Horvath (*reading it carefully*) Oh! This is so interesting for me . . .

Olley We do operate various discounts, of course.

Horvath reads. Garrard and Olley look at each other

Horvath (*as smiling and charming as ever*) These prices, they're so ridiculous! They're so much too high! I can buy German units, I can buy Swiss units for these prices!

Garrard German, Swiss—you won't get anything better.

Horvath Of course not. But if I buy German, if I buy Swiss, I get something delivered. From England, who knows? There will be strikes, perhaps, there will be inefficiency . . .

Garrard Look, as far as delivery dates go, I can give you my personal assurance . . .

Horvath Of course. Of course. And you'll give us a better price. All these things will be discussed. You'll write to this office in Budapest—(*He gives Garrard a card*)—and ask for the performance specification for this job. We'll send you the specification—you'll send us a tender—you'll give us better prices—and everything will be arranged.

Garrard How do we know our tender will be accepted?

Horvath Don't worry. Leave it to me. I'll look after it.

Olley Really?

Horvath Really!

Olley Well, that's very kind of you. Isn't it, John?

Horvath No, no, no—it's such a pleasure for me to meet people like you and do business with you. Because there is no-one in the world who is so charming to meet as an Englishman.

Olley I don't know what to say to that. Do you, John?

Horvath Don't say anything.

Olley Except, of course, to say that a *Hungarian* . . .

Horvath Please. Let me tell you something. We shall build the conference centre, and it will be a big success. A big success for me, and a big success for you. Because people will come from all over the world. They'll look at your walls, they'll say, but these are fantastic, these are world-beating, and it will be very important for you. Now, when you go back to London I want you to do one small thing for me.

Garrard Ah.

Horvath No, no, no—it's not like that. It's something very little.

The door opens a crack

No time, no trouble, no money. (*He turns sharply to look at the door*)

The door closes again

Someone wants to come in?

Olley goes to the door and throws it open

Olley Come in . . . Come in, come in!

Mrs Rogers enters. She has put on a long evening dress

Mrs Rogers I'm sorry. I don't want to interrupt if you're still . . .

Garrard (*to Mrs Rogers*) Sit down. (*To Horvath*) Go on, go on.

But Horvath is looking attentively at Mrs Rogers

Olley This is my secretary, Mrs Rogers.

Horvath Yes, we met when I arrived. But you've changed! You've put on this beautiful evening dress!

Mrs Rogers (*embarrassed*) Oh . . .

Horvath But the colour is perfect.

Mrs Rogers Thank you.

Horvath The same colour as your eyes.

Mrs Rogers Yes.

Horvath You're so young, but you wear it with such grace. (*To Olley*) I must compliment you. You have a most exquisite assistant.

Olley Yes . . . well . . . yes.

Horvath (*to Garrard*) You must envy your colleague's good fortune.

Garrard Yes . . . yes . . .

Horvath (*to Mrs Rogers*) But you're going out for the evening, and I'm keeping you waiting. You have some business here?

Mrs Rogers No, no.

Garrard (*to Mrs Rogers*) Just sit down. (*To Horvath*) So what do you want us to do?

Mrs Rogers sits down at her desk, trying to make herself as inconspicuous as during the working day

Horvath I'll tell you. (*To Mrs Rogers*) I've been having such an interesting conversation with these two gentlemen. I admire their products so much.

Garrard And you want us to do what?

Horvath No, no, I must be allowed to compliment you. Because I know how it is if you work in industry. No-one loves you! They tell you you're destroying the world. And in the end you start to believe it yourself!

Olley It is rather amazing, isn't it? They either take us for granted or they despise us.

Horvath So I want to tell you how important it is to make things. That's how man lives, by making. To be is to make. To make food, to make drink, to make shelter—yes, but also to make thought. Because to think is to make. It's so strange! Your critics consider themselves thinkers. But where are their thoughts? Their thoughts are nowhere, their thoughts are nothing; just ink on paper; dead leaves in the wind. But here are *your* thoughts! You can see them and touch them and turn them around and sell them to me. You're the real thinkers!

Olley I must say, a little flattery from time to time—it's as good as a fortnight in Majorca.

Horvath Flattery? That's not flattery! All right, it's flattery. But listen, I'll tell you something about flattery. Flattery is like insult—there must always be a particle of truth in it.

Garrard All right. Let's get back to business.

Horvath All right. My brother-in-law.

Garrard Oh, brother-in-law problem, is it? Wants a job, does he?

Horvath No, no, no, no. He has a job. A job is what he doesn't want. What he wants is to leave the job and sell cars.

Garrard Go on, go on.

Horvath Old cars.

Garrard Secondhand?

Horvath Very old cars. Bugattis, Hispano-Suizas.

Olley Vintage cars.

Horvath Vintage cars. He wants to buy them, he wants to sell them. He wants to find them hidden away in old farm buildings, clean them, make them work. This is his ambition. This is what he wants to make of his life.

Olley Do they have vintage car dealers in Hungary?

Horvath No.

Garrard So he wants to come to England?

Horvath Yes. And to come to England he must have a work permit from your Government.

Olley He'll never get a work permit as a vintage car dealer.

Horvath Of course not. To get a work permit there must be a job that needs special qualifications.

Garrard Has he got any qualifications?

Horvath Oh! He has wonderful qualifications!

Garrard What sort of qualifications?

Horvath He's a qualified dental technician!

Olley A dental technician?

Horvath At one of the biggest hospitals in Budapest.

Olley How would we persuade the Department of Employment we need a dental technician in a joinery works?

Horvath You're going to sell your products in Hungary? You must have a qualified expert in Hungarian health regulations!

Garrard (*to Olley*) Have we thought about the health angle?

Olley What health angle?

Garrard Don't know, do we, until we've got someone who understands the regulations.

Olley But we won't be *getting* someone who understands Hungarian health regulations! We'll be getting a secondhand car salesman! (*To Horvath*) Isn't that right?

Horvath You won't be getting anyone. You won't even see him.

Garrard (*to Olley*) So what's the problem? We're rescuing someone from Eastern Europe. Right up your street, isn't it?

Olley (*to Horvath*) Is he suffering political persecution?

Garrard Of course he's suffering political persecution! They won't let him be a secondhand car salesman!

Horvath Look, it's nothing. You just send a letter to the Department of Employment in London. (*He hands Garrard a piece of paper*) You see, I've written the address for you. And you say, "We wish to employ Mr Ferenc Paszka"—look, it's all here.

Garrard looks at the paper and broods

Garrard What do you think, then, Tom?

Olley You know what I think.

Garrard (*looking at his watch*) Well, we'll talk about it over dinner.

Olley John . . .

Garrard What?

Olley *I* can't talk about it over dinner because I have a dinner engagement already.

Garrard Well, that's all right. Dr Horvath and I—

Olley —will talk about it over dinner—of course, and a very fruitful discussion it will be, without me there to make difficulties—except that I believe you also have a dinner engagement already, don't you, John?

Garrard Me? Oh . . . (*He turns to Mrs Rogers*)

Mrs Rogers Oh, please—don't worry about me. I'll get something in the coffeeshop downstairs.

Horvath Oh, but you're taking this young lady out for dinner! How charming!

Garrard No, that's all right. She doesn't mind.

Horvath No, no, no! Pleasure before business! You discuss the question with your colleague. I'll come here in the morning. (*He shakes Mrs Rogers's hand*) Good-bye! It's been so nice to meet you. Have a wonderful dinner. (*He shakes hands with Olley*) Good-bye! I so much admire a man with real moral principles. (*He shakes hands with Garrard*) Good-bye, Mr Garrard. Everything you need—it's written on that piece of paper. Because we're going to put your walls in our conference centre, I'm sure of that, and they're going to be a big success. If we can just check those health regulations first.

Horvath exits with all his parcels

Garrard So what do you think?

Olley What do I think? I think you're a child! There's a window —here's a brick—and it's more than your soul's worth to resist putting the two together!

Garrard Uh-huh. But he's making a straight deal? Work permit —sale?

Olley I don't know what you *want*! I've watched you at work for thirty-two years, and I do not know what it is you're after! You don't care about right and wrong. But then you don't care about money or pleasure. You don't care about other people. But then you don't care about yourself. The only thing you care about is the window and the brick, the brick and the window. There's the dog—here's a tin can—and you just have to see what happens. You're a delinquent child, John! But you're not a child—you're fifty-four—you're a psychopath!

Garrard Tom, what are you fussing about now?

Olley You would, wouldn't you, though? You'd have quite happily left her to get herself a ham sandwich at the snack bar in her evening dress!

Garrard You *want* me to give her dinner? I don't know what you're on about, Tom. Five minutes ago you *didn't* want me to!

Olley But you've asked her now!

Mrs Rogers I'd really rather have a sandwich than this.

Olley No, he's made the deal. He's giving you dinner. Caviar— champagne—a floor show; the lot. You make sure you get it, too.

Mrs Rogers I'll wait outside.

Olley You wait right here.

Garrard All I want to know is what you think about *this*. (*He indicates the paper that Horvath gave him*)

Olley I think you're going ahead with it.

Garrard Not if you think we shouldn't.

Olley You know what I think. I think it's wrong.

Garrard You mean it won't work?

Olley It may well not work. They must have thought of tricks like this. We may easily find ourselves in court. But whether it works or not it's *wrong*. There is a purpose behind the law on work permits, John. It's to protect people's jobs.

Garrard Secondhand car salesmen?

Olley Anyway, it's wrong.

Garrard Tom, if you think it's wrong, that's that. (*He tears the paper up and throws it on the floor*)

Pause

Olley I'm sorry, John.

Garrard Wouldn't have worked.

Olley No. I wish it wasn't always me that put the brakes on, though.

Garrard Got to have brakes. Wouldn't get very far down the street without brakes.

Olley I shouldn't have got so worked up about it.

Garrard Always take your advice in the end, Tom.

Olley Sometimes.

Garrard Wouldn't have got very far in life without you.

Olley Oh well.

Pause

Garrard Slimy little devil, wasn't he?

Olley laughs, Garrard smiles

Olley Well, I'm off. Funny, though. *I* used to be a bit of a handful once. Before I met you. I got up on the roof of the control-tower one Mess night at Scampton and dropped a ten-pound can of strawberry jam over the edge just to see what happened when it hit the concrete.

Garrard Always going on about that bloody jam.

Olley This was in the middle of the war! Jam was on the ration! Criminal, really. Then there was the night we came back off an

op and found the tail-gunner fast asleep. Pennington, little
Penny Pennington. Poor old Penny, shut away on his own in
the dark back there all night. But he could have got us all
killed. So I said to the others, All right, then, he wants to
sleep—let him sleep. Be quite funny. He'll wake up—it'll be
pitch dark—he won't know where the hell he is. So we left him
out there on the perimeter track. Debriefed. Went to bed.

Garrard Never told me this one before.

Olley No.

Garrard So what happened?

Olley All came out at the court of inquiry. Hour or so later
little Penny wakes up. Can't see anything—can't hear anything. Just blackness and the sound of the wind. And the first
thing that comes into his head is, My God, we've been hit!
We've lost all four engines! We're in a glide! So he calls up the
rest of the crew on the intercom. "Skip ...? Mike ...?
Tom ...?" Nothing. Christ, he thinks, they've baled out and
left me here! So he bales out, too! (*He laughs: then stops*) Hits
the deck ten feet below instead of ten thousand feet, and breaks
both legs. And there he lay, fully conscious, until the ground
crew came on in the morning. No, I haven't told you that one
before. Well, take care, then. See you tomorrow.

Olley exits

Garrard broods. Mrs Rogers picks up the torn scraps of paper

Garrard What?

Mrs Rogers These bits of paper lying around. (*She takes them
back to her desk, where the wastepaper-basket is*)

Garrard I wonder what a ten-pound can of strawberry jam was
worth on the black market? (*He looks at his watch*) All right,
if we're going to eat, let's eat.

He ushers her impatiently towards the door

Mrs Rogers I'm getting quite hungry. I think I'm really just
going to sit back this evening and enjoy myself.

Garrard Press the button for the lift. I'll catch you up.

Mrs Rogers exits

Garrard turns back and begins to search through the wastepaper-basket

  Mrs Rogers enters. She watches him

Mrs Rogers If you're looking for those bits of paper . . .
Garrard Where are they, then?
Mrs Rogers (*indicating her handbag*) I've got them in here for you.

Garrard gazes at her for a moment, then puts the wastepaper-basket down and ushers her towards the door

Garrard Eat, eat, eat . . . (*He turns out all the lights*)

  Mrs Rogers and Garrard exit.

                              CURTAIN

ACT II

The same

Darkness
Mrs Rogers and Garrard enter. He turns the lights on. She is carrying a very large, whimsical, cuddly toy. He closes the door and stands gazing at her, absorbed

Garrard Buddhism?
Mrs Rogers You look quite startled.
Garrard You mean you're a Buddhist?
Mrs Rogers Well, I go to the classes.
Garrard You're not serious about it?
Mrs Rogers I'm very interested in it.
Garrard Buddhism!
Mrs Rogers It's not as surprising as all that.

Pause. He gazes at her

Have you ever thought of going to evening classes? You could learn a language. It's a very good way of taking your mind off things.
Garrard And what, you believe in it all, do you?
Mrs Rogers We've been talking about me the whole evening. You haven't told me anything about yourself at all.
Garrard But you think there's something in it?
Mrs Rogers I really ought to be going. It's after eleven.
Garrard Sit down, sit down. (*He draws the curtains and turns various lights on, trying to get a more intimate effect*)
Mrs Rogers Well . . .
Garrard You're going to have a drink.
Mrs Rogers Oh, no, I won't. Not for me. Thank you. It was a lovely evening, though. I did enjoy it.
Garrard But you're seriously interested in this Buddhism stuff, are you? Sit down.

Pause

Mrs Rogers (*sitting on the sofa*) We need some kind of meaning in life, don't we? We can't go on like this.

Garrard Like what?

Mrs Rogers Well, just concerned with . . . all this.

Garrard What, the product?

Mrs Rogers Well, material things. I just feel all this is irrelevant in some way. We're trying to escape from—well, from ourselves. Don't you ever feel that?

He thinks

Garrard Every Tuesday evening?

Mrs Rogers What?

Garrard The classes.

Mrs Rogers Yes. I started last September.

Garrard Where you meet this gentleman friend of yours, is it?

Mrs Rogers Yes.

Garrard That's what got you interested?

Mrs Rogers In the first place.

Garrard So you just see him on Tuesdays?

Mrs Rogers Tuesdays and Fridays.

Garrard Why—there's another class on Fridays?

Mrs Rogers His wife has a class.

Garrard So you two go out for a meal together?

Mrs Rogers No, he comes round for the evening.

Garrard What do you do? Talk about nothingness?

Mrs Rogers How do you mean?

Garrard Nirvana?

Mrs Rogers I don't think nirvana is really nothingness.

Pause

Garrard What's his wife's class?

Mrs Rogers Commercial French.

Pause

Garrard What *is* it all about, then?

Mrs Rogers What, Buddhism? Well, it's all based on something called the Four Noble Truths.

Garrard Go on.

Mrs Rogers Oh, I couldn't explain them. You'd have to ask someone who really knew about it.

Garrard Why—they're difficult, are they?
Mrs Rogers I think all Buddhist ideas are quite difficult.
Garrard You mean I wouldn't understand them?
Mrs Rogers They're difficult even for Buddhists to understand.
Garrard Let's have a go.

Mrs Rogers rises and looks at her watch

Mrs Rogers I think perhaps I should . . .
Garrard Sit down.

Pause. Mrs Rogers sits

Mrs Rogers Tell me something about yourself, then.
Garrard Why? What do you want to know?
Mrs Rogers Aren't you going to sit down?
Garrard Asking too many questions, am I?
Mrs Rogers I don't mind. But it can't be very relaxing for you.
You couldn't have worked harder if I'd been a customer.
Though of course you live for your work.
Garrard Don't you?
Mrs Rogers I quite enjoy it. Or at any rate I enjoy getting it
done. No, that's not right. As soon as I've got the work done I
forget I ever did it. What I like is being just about to get it
done. I sit there and I think, just this one more letter to do and
I'll have done the lot. And I put the paper in the typewriter
quite slowly, to make the feeling last. Or I'm halfway through,
and I think, isn't that nice—only the same distance again to go.
Or I'm right at the beginning even, and I think, I've only got
so much to do, and then I'll be in the middle, and when I'm in
the middle I'll only have the same amount still in front of me—
in fact slightly *less*, because then I'll be on to that lovely final
letter. So, yes, I suppose I do like work. And there it is, every
day. It saw me through, after my husband left me. They all go
sooner or later, don't they, the people you rely on. But the
work stays. Day after day. Year after year. Work in the office,
work at home. (*She laughs*) Sometimes you feel it's taking you
over completely! Specially when you live alone. When I make
myself supper in the evening I always cook myself a proper
meal, and I always try to make sure I really enjoy it. I wouldn't
enjoy it if I knew I'd still got all the washing up to do. So I

wash up everything I can in the kitchen as I go along, and I put
the meal on a tray so I can just pop it back in the kitchen
afterwards and wash the last bits and pieces up in the morning
with the breakfast things. But the trouble is, when I do sit
down with the tray in my lap what I'm thinking is, Well, I've
just got this little bit of eating to do and then I can put the tray
back in the kitchen. In fact there was one famous occasion—I
took the tray into the living-room to eat, and then I just
slipped back into the kitchen for a moment to wipe up some
wet marks I'd noticed on the work-top. And when I'd finished
wiping the work-top I thought, Well, that's that, that's all done
for tonight. I'll have a bath and get to bed early for once. Then
about one o'clock I woke up with a terrible nagging feeling.
And do you know, it wasn't even hunger? It was just worry
because I knew there was something I'd forgotten to do.
(*Pause*) I suppose if we'd had children . . . (*Pause*) I felt a bit
small, sitting there in the middle of the night eating congealed
lamb chop.

Garrard (*sitting by her*) So you're what, you're in love with this
pal of yours, are you?

Mrs Rogers (*laughing*) All the girls I know complain that men
only want to talk about themselves.

Garrard He wants to talk about himself, does he?

Mrs Rogers He's just one of the lonely ones.

Garrard Like you.

Mrs Rogers Yes. And you.

Garrard I'm lonely, am I?

Mrs Rogers Aren't you?

Garrard (*beginning to run his thumb over the back of her hand*)
Nice hands.

Mrs Rogers Thank you.

Garrard Look after them, do you? Put stuff on at night?

Mrs Rogers Just hand cream. Your thumb's quite hard and
rough. You're not a gardener, are you?

*He runs his thumb over her forearm. She watches it, completely
passive*

Garrard Put it on your arms as well?

Mrs Rogers Sometimes.

Garrard Where do you stop?

Mrs Rogers At my elbows. Look, you don't have to do this, you
 know. It was a nice evening. I enjoyed it very much. You don't
 have to do anything else.
Garrard You do your face, though.
Mrs Rogers Yes.
Garrard Face and neck.
Mrs Rogers Yes.
Garrard What's that—face cream?
Mrs Rogers Moisturizing cream.

He runs his thumb over her shin and calf

Garrard Four of them, are there?
Mrs Rogers Four Noble Truths, yes.
Garrard What's the first one?
Mrs Rogers You'll only be disappointed.
Garrard Come on.

Pause

Mrs Rogers The first one just says that there is suffering everywhere.

Pause

   That's all. I'm putting it in my own words. I can't remember
 the proper technical term for suffering.
Garrard Suffering everywhere?
Mrs Rogers I did warn you.

*He turns back her skirt and rubs his thumb over her knees. She
watches passively, as before*

Garrard Nice knees.
Mrs Rogers Thank you.
Garrard Put anything on them?
Mrs Rogers No.
Garrard What's the second one?
Mrs Rogers I'm not telling you.

*He takes her leg and lifts it into his lap. He runs his thumb up and
down the length of it, from the knee to the ankle, absorbed*

   I suppose you're a great womanizer. Just like a business
 opportunity. Once you've noticed it you can't let it pass.

Garrard What's the second one?
Mrs Rogers You're not supposed to make love to the secretaries.
Garrard Aren't you?

He takes her shoe off

Mrs Rogers You know you're not.
Garrard Get a caning from Tom, would I?
Mrs Rogers You don't need to ask Mr Olley.
Garrard What's the second one?
Mrs Rogers It's not right.

He takes her other shoe off, and runs his hand slowly back to her knee

The second truth is that suffering is caused by desire, and the third truth is that suffering ends only when you get rid of desire. I think when it says desire it means any expression of your own individual self instead of the universal self. It means trying to find pleasure in your separateness from everything around you, trying to use the world instead of being a part of it. What the Third Truth is saying is that our suffering will end only when we achieve a state of nirvana . . .

There is a muffled thump at the main door. Garrard looks round. Faint giggles are heard outside. The handle is tried. Garrard gets up and crosses to the door. Mrs Rogers takes her shoes and flees back to the safety of the desk on the stand where she works during the day. Garrard flings the door open

On the threshold stands Anni, with Prosser behind her. They are both in a rather insanely ebullient mood, though Prosser is for the moment quietened down by the sight of Garrard. He remains in the doorway while Anni rushes in. Neither Anni nor Prosser notices Mrs Rogers

Anni You see? He's awake! I knew this! He never sleeps! We were standing outside the door listening are you asleep or not.
Prosser I tried to stop her.
Anni We've come to bring you to the party. Everyone's there! They all want to meet you! Because Frank and I we've told them everything about you—but *everything!* Such funny stories! When they were burning your friend in the crematorium! And—oh, I don't know—but so *funny!* But then we don't

know what to say, because Frank says "I don't know anything *about* this man!" So I think, but this is just crazy, they must meet him! So we jumped into a taxi . . .

Prosser I couldn't stop her.

Anni Because you're only in Frankfurt for one night, and really and truly it's crazy for you to sit up here all sad and lonely, when we're all happy and together, and you know what, we could dance, we could just be crazy, because listen, I've got some terrible strange desire to put my arms round you and kiss you.

Prosser She wants to take your shoes off.

Anni Sh! That should be a secret!

Garrard (*to Prosser*) I thought you were having dinner with Verhaeren?

Prosser begins to shake irregularly

What? What?

Anni Mr Verhaeren!

At this Prosser can control his laughter no longer. He comes into the room and collapses into a chair. He and Anni both laugh helplessly

Prosser I'm sorry—I'm sorry . . .

Anni It was the look on Mr Verhaeren's face!

Prosser Very slightly drunk, I'm afraid, Mr Garrard . . .

Anni But it was the look on his face when the police arrested him!

Garrard Arrested him? Verhaeren?

Prosser (*pulling himself together*) I'm sorry. Disgraceful state. I really am rather . . .

Garrard What happened?

Prosser Yes, what happened?

Anni (*to Prosser*) We saw you. In the Kaiserstrasse.

Prosser (*to Garrard*) Me and Verhaeren. We'd just come out of the restaurant.

Anni (*to Garrard*) Christian and I were in this demonstration. Christian is my boy friend. So policemen, policemen, policemen—and suddenly, there's Mr Prosser! So I shout, "Mr Prosser!" And I wave to him like this, and he waves back . . .

Prosser And the next thing I know, someone's trying to break my arm.

Anni So now Mr Prosser knows what the police are like! And he gets angry, and he kicks the policeman, and they arrest Mr Verhaeren!

Anni and Prosser are both overcome with laughter again

Garrard So Verhaeren's now in the cells?

Anni No! Christian and some other men pull him back, and we all run like chickens, and the police chase us all the way up the Weserstrasse, and do you know Mr Prosser has never in his life before been chased by the police?

Prosser I was terrified.

Anni Yes, because they're all angry, they're all shouting, they want to kill us, but it's wonderful, because we can run faster than the police, and afterwards you feel so good! You're breathing and breathing, and you just want to laugh and put your arms round everyone!

Garrard So where's Verhaeren now?

Anni He's with all these people at the party.

Prosser And if you think *I'm* drunk you want to see *him!*

Garrard And what do you reckon—he's coming through with an order tomorrow or not?

Anni (*delighted*) Oh! We tell him all these things, and what he thinks is just will Mr Verhaeren make an order! This is really beautiful!

Prosser (*suddenly melancholy*) No, it's not. It's heartbreaking.

Garrard Well, is he or isn't he?

Prosser Listen, John—Mr Garrard—I'm going to tell you something.

Garrard Just tell me yes or no.

Prosser Listen.

Anni Yes, listen to him.

Prosser All right, I know I'm a bit drunk. I wouldn't be saying it otherwise. So just listen a moment.

Garrard Right, then, I'm listening.

Prosser No, listen, listen.

Anni He is listening.

Garrard Come on.

Prosser You're missing the point. You're missing the whole huge, tiny point.

Anni The point of what?

Prosser The point of what? The point of everything! You want
to know what the point is? I'll tell you what the point is. The
whole point of life, John, is to . . . How can I explain it if you
can't see it for yourself? The whole point of life . . . Wait, wait,
wait. Now I've got started I'm going to say it, even if I never
say another word. The whole point of life is this. It's to stand on
the edge and take a deep breath and . . . Listen, do you know
what Anni and I have been doing for the past half-hour?

Garrard Getting one of our customers arrested.

Prosser After that.

Garrard Telling him what the point of life is.

Prosser No, no, this isn't for anyone else. This is just for you,
John. Anni and I have been sitting out on the stairs at this
party and we have been . . .

Anni (*laughing and covering her face*) Oh, *no!*

Prosser No, I'm going to tell him. We have been sitting out on
the stairs—everyone else in the kitchen shouting their heads
off—no-one can hear us—and we've been singing Beethoven
bloody symphonies!

*He begins singing, and conducting, a section from the last move-
ment of the Seventh Symphony—the second subject, from bar
fifty-two onwards. Anni joins in*

Boom badoom badoom badoom ba*doom* badoom badoom
badoom . . . Seventy people! Seventy mad musicians! All mad
together! All on the beat, all on the chord, all going like the
demons of hell! Just the thought of it's enough to lift the roof
off your head! *Boom* badoom badoom badoom ba*doom*
badoom badoom badoom . . . You ask me if I'm sitting there
thinking, is this B flat major? No, I'm not! I'm not sitting there
thinking anything! I'm sitting there as empty as an empty
room and everything inside me from my brain to my liver to
my toenails is going *Boom* badoom badoom badoom ba*doom*
badoom badoom badoom . . . I'm not sitting there at all! I'm
standing in the air a mile above the ground, and everything in
the whole wide world is going *Boom* badoom badoom badoom
ba*doom* badoom badoom badoom . . . And all I want to do is
to put my head back and stretch out my arms and give thanks.
And the only reason I care that it's Symphony Number Seven
in A Major, opus ninety-two, is that I want to talk to everyone

about it, like Colin Hewlett talking about his wife and children, and there's nothing nothing nothing you can say about it except to say its name, which is the Seventh Symphony, or just the Seventh, or possibly Opus ninety-two, or the A major symphony, except just once in a while when you're drunk enough to be honest and you've met the right person and you can go *Boom* badoom badoom badoom ba*doom* badoom badoom badoom . . . So all right, we sit in here all day and we worry away about abura and afrormosia, and agba, and orders from Belgium, and who's going to have the agency in Saudi Arabia, and extruded chipboard and inert European flax-board—(*referring to the toy*)—and what the hell is this?—we're marketing sponge-rubber yellow Yogi bears now?

Mrs Rogers That's mine.

Prosser and Anni see her for the first time

Prosser God God. The lovely Mrs R. Lurking in the shadows.

Anni You don't still work?

Mrs Rogers Could I have it, please?

Prosser This is yours?

Mrs Rogers Please.

Prosser Where in the world did you get it?

Mrs Rogers There was a man selling them outside the restaurant.

Prosser And you bought it? You paid money for this?

Garrard I bought it.

Anni (*realizing*) Oh . . .!

Prosser (*oblivious*) So all right, we spend half the night going to expensive restaurants and buying huge platefuls of steak for people who mean nothing to us, and large cigars, and sponge-yellow Yogi bears, and that's fine, I'm not criticizing, I enjoy the work, I'm all in favour of it. But . . .

Anni Frank . . .

Prosser Where was I? Where did all this start?

Anni We must say good night.

Prosser Oh, the point. Yes, if you want to know what the point of it all is, I'll tell you in words of one syllable—it's *Boom* badoom badoom badoom ba*doom* badoom badoom badoom . . .

Garrard You'll have its arms off if you thump it up and down like that.

Anni (*gently taking the bear from Prosser*) It's beautiful.

Prosser (*a doubt beginning to trouble him*) Just a moment. If you bought that thing for Goetz . . .

Anni (*kisses it*) Beautiful sleepy bear. (*She gives it to Mrs Rogers*)

Mrs Rogers Thank you.

Prosser realizes and is chastened

Prosser Oh, bloody hell.

Anni (*to Prosser*) Come on.

Garrard You just make sure Verhaeren gets back to his hotel tonight.

Prosser Yes. Right. I'm sorry, Mr Garrard. I didn't realize it was a present. The bear. As a present it's good.

Anni Oh! I'm so happy! I'm so happy for both of you! (*She runs back and kisses first Garrard and then Mrs Rogers*) Good night, bear. Sleep well. (*She runs back to the door*)

Garrard Oh, and Frank.

Prosser Yes?

Garrard Is he?

Prosser Is he what?

Garrard Going to?

Prosser gazes at Garrard for some moments

Prosser Yes, if we can guarantee our sound reduction figures.

Anni and Prosser exit

Mrs Rogers sits down and hugs the bear. Pause

Garrard Embarrassed?

Mrs Rogers Yes.

Pause. Then he gives a brief laugh

What?

Garrard So was I.

Mrs Rogers (*surprised*) Really?

Garrard A bit.

Pause

Mrs Rogers (*gently*) Good.

Pause

Garrard You never told me the fourth one.

Mrs Rogers No.

Pause

Garrard (*sitting down beside her*) So what's the fourth one?
Mrs Rogers It's a secret.
Garrard Let's get it over with
Mrs Rogers No.
Garrard The first three were terrible.
Mrs Rogers Exactly.
Garrard Got them in a cracker you'd take the crackers back.
Mrs Rogers I expect you would.
Garrard So what's the fourth one?

Mrs Rogers shakes her head and smiles. She goes on shaking her head and smiling and hugging the bear as Garrard leans closer and closer

What, it's the real stuff, is it? Come on, what is it? No treading on beetles? Something like that? Stand on your head every day? Don't kiss the girls? Come on, come on, come on, come on . . .

The telephone rings. Pause

Mrs Rogers Leave it. Can't you leave it?

Garrard goes to the telephone and picks up the receiver. Mrs Rogers strokes the bear

Garrard (*into the telephone*) Yes? . . . Where are you? . . . (*He looks at his watch*) No . . . Right . . . (*He puts the receiver down*)
Mrs Rogers Peter Davis?
Garrard Downstairs.
Mrs Rogers He's coming up, is he?
Garrard I might have known.

Silence. Garrard thinks

Mrs Rogers I'll go, then.
Garrard What's he up to?
Mrs Rogers It's nearly midnight.
Garrard He'll just have finished dinner with Talbot. Now he's coming straight round to talk to me.
Mrs Rogers He wouldn't really sell this firm to British Paper. Would he?

Garrard I'll start up again in something.

Mrs Rogers Why don't you wait to see what he says?

Garrard I'll take my handshake and start up somewhere. Won't retire, I'll tell you that. Couldn't. Go mad. Be dead inside a year.

Mrs Rogers It's probably about something else altogether. I hope it's all right. I'm sure it will be.

Garrard Sit down, sit down.

Mrs Rogers No, it was a lovely evening, and I'm very grateful, and anyway I've got my bear to remind me and keep me company . . .

There is a knock at the door. Mrs Rogers looks at it, and then at Garrard

Garrard Sit down as far as I'm concerned.

She shakes her head

Embarrass you?

She nods. Garrard opens the bedroom door for her. Another knock

Mrs Rogers exits into the bedroom

Garrard opens the main door

Davis enters. He is in his early forties, a man of apparently profound ordinariness in every way except for the completeness of his repose

Davis On second thoughts I agree with you about the Bletchley site. We'll take Trafford Park off you instead. You'll sell it to Leslie at the 1976 valuation, and they'll lease it back to you at current rentals. In a full year we should be able to wipe another hundred thousand off your taxable profits. As far as this year goes, we'll simply bill you a hundred thousand for head office and management services.

Garrard Management services? What management services?

Davis Our services in getting a hundred thousand off your profits for you. So Ridgways have got that Nigerian business.

Garrard Three hundred thousand installed. Fixed price. They'll lose money on it.

Davis You got anything?

Garrard University of Tripoli.

Davis You got that in London.

Garrard We'll announce it here.

Davis What else?

Garrard We're chasing a couple. Fair-sized. Hundred-plus.

Davis So nothing?

Garrard We're not selling brushes.

Davis And you're happy, are you?

Garrard What, with the results here? Ask me in six months time.

Davis You don't look happy.

Garrard So what, you want to sit down, you want a drink?

Davis And it's not the state of the order-book that's worrying you?

Garrard Nothing's worrying me.

Davis Seven per cent interim, nine per cent coming up—you should be laughing all over your face.

Garrard Scotch? Brandy?

Davis It's not work that kills people like us, John, it's worry. No, thanks. I never worry. I switch on, concentrate, switch off. I haven't lost a night's sleep in ten years. Six hours a night. Never more, never less, never take pills. Do you sleep?

Garrard I thought you were in Brussels.

Davis (*sitting*) So what's the worry, John?
So what's the worry, John?

Garrard (*walking about*) Nothing's the worry. What did Ronnie Talbot have to say?

Davis Ronnie Talbot?

Garrard You've just had dinner with him.

Davis Got your spies out, have you, John?

Garrard Let's get down to it.

Davis John . . . Sit down. I can't talk to you while you're walking up and down like that.

Garrard stops walking

Garrard What is it, then?

Davis Sit down . . . Sit down.

Garrard sits

John, you must learn to make yourself relax. I'm serious. You're going to kill yourself.

Garrard (*jumping up*) Yes, yes, yes, yes. So let's get to the point.
Davis Sit down!

Garrard sits

> Now, unclench your muscles. Feet—legs—arms—neck—the
> neck's important. Stomach . . . Look, we both work hard.
> We've both had a long day. But I can sit here at my ease. You
> see? Absolutely still. Not a muscle moving. I can wait—say
> nothing—just think—not even think . . .

*Silence. Garrard leans back but one hand continues to twitch
impatiently*

> Got a cat at home?

Garrard A cat?
Davis Get yourself a cat, John, and study it. Pounce—just like
you. Then—nothing. Soft as a cushion till next time.

Silence

> Don't like me, do you?

Garrard I'll tell you whether I like you when I know what you're
up to.
Davis I like you, John. Like the way you work. Whole business
inside your head. Materials, unions, sales. Sales above all. I
admire that. Eyes fixed on tomorrow and next week and next
month and next year. That's right. That's good . . . No, wait,
wait, wait, wait! We haven't got there yet. You get the stuff
made and you get it sold, and I can't help liking you for that,
because where should I be without you? I'd be in there making
it myself. I'd be out there travelling it!
Garrard So what, he didn't make an offer?
Davis Ronnie? Yes, he made an offer.
Garrard How much?
Davis One pound twenty a share.
Garrard One twenty?
Davis Cash, John, cash.
Garrard They're worth three!
Davis He'd go to one sixty, one seventy, if we were serious.
Garrard One seventy? What, to close us down?
Davis Not very good, is it?
Garrard It must be worth more to him than that!

Davis No. You know why not? You might find this interesting,
John. He thinks the firm's you and you're the firm. And he
thinks you'll be in a nursing home within a year or two anyway.

Garrard (*jumping up*) So what, you told him what he could do
with it?

Davis Sit down, John, sit down. Every time you jump up like
that you're wiping another thousand pounds off the Group's
holding in you. Sit down!

Garrard (*sitting*) You're trying something on, I know that.

Davis If you just listen I'll tell you. First of all I'm going to get
you a thorough medical check-up. When was the last time you
had one?

Garrard Last winter. Then what?

Davis If the report's all right I might have another go at
Ronnie ... Relax! Lean back! Neck—stomach—let them
go ... Look, John, you know what the Group's liquidity
situation is. If I could get what, two forty, two fifty for you
cash down, I'd sell you to the cat's meat man. But if I can't,
you're more use to me inside the Group. Because my problem
is this. I've got four companies in the Group making building
components, and only one of them making money. Your
company. So what I want to do, John, if you'll agree—and this
is why I've come round to have a word with you tonight—I
want to bracket all four companies together as a Building
Components Division, and put the whole division in the hands
of someone who's a proved success in the building components
field. Someone who really knows how to get the stuff made and
get it sold. So this is what I'm saying: Managing Director of
the Building Components Division, with a seat on the main
board—we'll talk about money back in London—and I'd
really like to get it sorted out before the board meeting on
Tuesday.

Garrard thinks

What are you looking worried about now? *I'll* pay for the
champagne.

Garrard Four firms making building components? You've only
got two. There's me, there's Ted Shaw. No-one else.

Davis There's Heritage.

Garrard Heritage? Heritage don't make building components. They make brass fancy goods.

Davis They make building components.

Garrard What? Candlesticks, hearth-sets, cocktail trolleys . . .

Davis They also make period brassmongery for door furnishing. I count them as a building components firm.

Garrard What's the fourth one, then?

Davis George Playfair.

Garrard Playfair? They install netball pitches!

Davis They build sports facilities. They supply the components to build sports facilities.

Garrard Only one thing Ted Shaw and Heritage and Playfair have got in common—they all make losses.

Davis It's a challenge, John. If I can't stop you worrying, I'll give you something to worry about.

Garrard Candlesticks?

Davis Door furnishings.

Garrard I can't sell candlesticks!

Davis You can sell door furnishings.

Garrard What do I know about netball courts?

Davis You'll find out. I know you, John. You'll be out there playing on them.

Garrard (*jumping up*) So what, this is really just a bit of gardening on the Group's accounts, is it?

Davis One profit looks better than three losses.

Garrard I won't be showing a profit. I'll be showing a loss.

Davis For a start. But then one loss looks better than three.

Garrard Particularly if it's mine instead of yours.

Davis You're on your feet again, John.

Garrard continues to walk up and down

All right, it's not your birthday—I'm not giving you a present. We're doing business—I'm offering you a deal. Something in it for me. Something in it for you.

Garrard And what, if I refuse, you go back to Ronnie Talbot, do you?

Davis Feel very aggrieved, don't you, John? Here you are, doing fine, taking your chipboard and turning it into a profit. And that's the complete game, as far as you're concerned. Nine per cent—you've done it, you're there. But your profit is where *my* game starts. I use your profit to create expectations of more. Expectations—that's *my* product. That's what brings in *my* profit. You're doing fine up in your small corner—and here am I picking you up and shifting you round the board like a chess piece. But what I'm offering, John, is to give you some pieces of your own. Show you how to play chess yourself. (*He rises*) You'll be back in London tomorrow? I'll give you a buzz. I want to get this in front of the board on Tuesday.

Garrard Ted Shaw?

Davis What about him?

Garrard He's one of the pieces?

Davis Not good enough for you?

Garrard *You* couldn't do anything with him.

Davis Take him off the table, then. Put him back in the box.

Garrard He's not the only one.

Davis No, and then there's me. You'll never be happy while I'm around.

Garrard So what, I put you back in the box, do I?

Davis You'll be on the main board. Vote me off.

Garrard Get a majority, would I?

Davis If I don't show them some results.

Garrard So then they give me the job? Is that what you're telling me? Or are you wagering I'll be dead before I cause you any trouble?

Davis Tomorrow, then. I'll ring you at home in the evening, nine, ten o'clock. (*He pulls back the curtain and looks out of the window*) Everything looks better from above, John. Even Frankfurt. All right, then, I'll leave you to get on with it.

Garrard Get on with what?

Davis I've been sitting on someone's handbag for the last ten minutes. Don't overdo it, though. I need another two years out of you yet.

Davis exits

Garrard opens the bedroom door, and then crosses to the window. He gazes out

Mrs Rogers enters, still holding her bear

Mrs Rogers Bad, was it?

No reaction; Garrard is brooding

Is he selling us?

No reaction. Mrs Rogers waits, then picks up her handbag and crosses to the main door

Anyway, you'll come out on top, whatever happens. You know that.

Garrard Fancy brassware!

Pause. Mrs Rogers waits at the door, to see if there is more to come

Horse brasses and warming pans! What can I do with stuff like that? Goal-posts and cricket-stumps! I'm not in that market—never have been—don't know it—not going to start now.

Pause. Mrs Rogers waits patiently

Four companies? How can I run four companies? I'm up into the small hours running one!

Pause

Mrs Rogers Mr Davis wants you to take more on?

Garrard How can I? I'd have to get somebody else to run this firm for a start. Who could I get? There's no-one! Don't tell me Tom! Tom couldn't run a Boy Scout jumble sale! If I wasn't here to watch him all the time he'd put the takings in the poor box.

Mrs Rogers I suppose there's . . .

Garrard Yes, there's Sydney Laver sitting up there in Manchester. You might as well say the girl who brings the tea round. I'd take Ian Weatherall in preference to Sydney Laver, and I wouldn't take Ian Weatherall, because what does Ian Weatherall know about the production side? I'm being made use of, aren't I? That's what sticks in my throat. I'm going to spend the rest of my life selling brass toasting-forks just to keep Davis on his feet. And where *are* his feet? On my neck! (*Pause*) You going or staying? Going, are you?

Mrs Rogers I'll stay if you want to talk.

Pause

Garrard Poetic justice, is that it?

Mrs Rogers I wasn't thinking that.

Garrard Some people like being used. That's their life. That's
what keeps them moving.

Mrs Rogers Possibly.

Garrard *You* like it.

Mrs Rogers Do I?

Garrard Don't you?

Mrs Rogers It doesn't matter about me.

Garrard Been sitting in there brooding about it, have you?

Pause

Mrs Rogers I was thinking about nirvana. You said nirvana
was nothingness. But that's not right at all. I wish I could
explain it to you. People usually say it's the self merging with
the rest of the universe. But the man who runs the classes says
it's more as if everything else was being absorbed into the self.
People think Buddhism is against the self. But it's not; it's just
against the wrong idea of the self as being separate. The man
who runs the classes says you have to imagine a raindrop
falling in a clear sky, completely filled with light from the
whole world round it.

Garrard I ought to be a raindrop? That what you're telling me?

Mrs Rogers We didn't really talk, did we. You just asked
questions. You just felt me to see what I felt like, and to see
whether I'd let you, and if Mr Davis hadn't arrived you'd have
made love to me, just to see whether it gave me pleasure, and
whether I was grateful, and I'm not complaining, I *should* have
been grateful—it would have been better than going to bed
with supper still sitting on the tray.

Garrard (*putting his arm round her*) All hurt, are you?

Mrs Rogers does not respond; she becomes more and more agitated

Mrs Rogers It's no good. We all play up to you. We all help you
to keep up this performance.

Garrard Me you're worrying about, is it?

Mrs Rogers I can't bear to watch.

Garrard Working too hard?

Mrs Rogers You won't look at yourself. You look at everything
but yourself. I can't think what it must be like, being inside that
shell. I'd like to help you come out, but you won't, and there's
nothing I can do to make you. It's useless to go on talking

about it, so I'll go away now, before I start to cry. You wouldn't like that. But I can't bear it, I don't know how to put up with my life. (*She picks up her bag and goes to the door*)

Garrard Just a moment . . .

Mrs Rogers No. No.

Garrard The name . . .

Mrs Rogers No. No. No.

Garrard The paper . . .

Mrs Rogers (*stopping*) What?

Garrard In your bag. You never gave it to me.

She walks back to Garrard without understanding, as if she had given in to entreaties to stay, and gazes at him

Where is it, where is it? If I'm going to be stuck with Ted Shaw under me then he can do something useful. He can offer that bloke's brother-in-law a job in Securex, and Tom'll never even hear about it.

Pause. Then she begins to hit him with the bear. The blows are hard. She is hysterical. He protects himself as best he can

Garrard What? What?

Mrs Rogers Hate. Hate. Hate. Can't live. My life.

Garrard (*trying to take the bear*) Give me that.

Mrs Rogers Destroying.

Garrard Give it.

Mrs Rogers Killing.

Garrard Give it.

Mrs Rogers Nothing.

Garrard Give it.

Mrs Rogers Nothing.

Garrard Give it.

Mrs Rogers No.

She holds the bear behind her. Garrard reaches around her for it. The scuffle slowly subsides into an embrace

Garrard Feel you breathing.

Pause

Feel your heart beating.

She drops the bear and her bag. Garrard begins to undress her

Mrs Rogers Wait.

She breaks free, goes to the door and checks that it is locked, goes to the telephone and takes the receiver off. Garrard watches her. One by one she turns off the lights. She opens the bedroom door and turns on the light inside. Then she turns off the last of the switches in the main room, so that the only light is now inside the bedroom

> *Garrard ushers her into the bedroom and follows her. The door is closed. Darkness. Pause*

Garrard (*off—an abstracted, amplified murmur*) Eastern Europe. Get into Eastern Europe. Hold Davis off if we get into Eastern Europe. Get that address if we get into Eastern Europe. Get into Eastern Europe if we get into Eastern Europe.

The display is illuminated

> *Horvath and Hewlett are standing on it. Horvath is demonstrating it to Hewlett, not by moving the walls, but by opening the doors and leading Hewlett through them*

Horvath Thirty minutes. These are all thirty-minute doors. Thirty minutes fire-resistance to get through all these doors into Eastern Europe . . .

> *Horvath and Hewlett exit through one of the doors in the display. Simultaneously, Shaw and Anni enter through another of the doors. He is demonstrating the display to her*

Shaw . . . Or sixty minutes of inert European flaxboard. The answer is to open the inert European flaxboard and go through into the Eastern European flaxboard . . .

> *Shaw and Anni exit. Simultaneously Hewlett and Davis appear through another door. From now on the doors of the display are in constant motion as people appear and disappear and reappear in different combinations of salesman and customer*

Hewlett (*to Davis*) . . . because if you're on the flaxboard you can always vote him off. Then we can buy the flaxboard off you at the 1843 valuation, and go through the accounts into Eastern Avenue.

Horvath (*to Shaw*) Eastern Avenue? Eastern Avenue leads through the main board into Eastern Bletchley, but the wonderful thing for you would be to go through *your* board into Eastern Euston . . .

Anni (*to Davis*) . . . And if we get into Eastern Euston in time, we can get a train at the 1928 valuation, which of course is 2028 in Eastern Euston time . . .

Davis (*to Hewlett*) And that brings us back to the same problem, which is to unbutton her outer doors and penetrate into the inner parts of Euston Avenue . . .

Shaw We're nearly there . . .

Horvath Nearly got it . . .

Anni Just going to . . .

Davis Just about to . . .

Hewlett Just on the point of . . .

Anni Just go through . . .

Shaw And this is the answer . . .

Horvath We've got the answer . . .

Hewlett The answer is if we can just . . .

Shaw Just . . .

Horvath Just . . .

Davis Just go through . . .

Anni Into Western Euston . . .

The bedroom door opens. As it does so, the lighting on the display is extinguished, leaving the room in darkness

Garrard stands in the bedroom doorway, silhouetted by a dim light from within. He enters, fumbles for the switch, and turns on the light. He is wearing pyjama trousers

The display is uninhabited, and Garrard does not look at it. He rubs his head, turns this way and that, trying to shake off the dream. He picks up papers from the desk, glances at them, and drops them before he has had time to read anything. On the floor near the sofa he finds Mrs Rogers's handbag, lying where she dropped it when he began to undress her. He picks it up and is about to open it when he hears a movement in the bedroom. He puts the bag back on the floor

Mrs Rogers enters from the bedroom, tying Garrard's dressing-gown about her. She stands at the door, watching Garrard

He glances up at her. She smiles tenderly at him. He continues to move restlessly about. As he passes her, he runs his hand through her hair abstractedly. She captures the hand and kisses it. He moves on

Garrard All right, then. What's the fourth one?

She sits down and makes him sit down as well. They sit facing each other, she holding his hand and stroking it, he sombre and attentive

Mrs Rogers (*gently*) The Fourth Noble Truth is the Noble Eightfold Path. Now of course you're going to ask me what the Noble Eightfold Path is, and I can't remember exactly what all the eight bits are. But they're things like Right Understanding and Right Action. Right Understanding means knowing things like, well, like the Four Noble Truths.

Garrard That's the Fourth Noble Truth? That you have to know the Four Noble Truths?

Mrs Rogers You have to know other things as well. You have to know the Five Groups of Human Attributes, and the Twelve Spokes of the Wheel of Life, and the Three Signs of Being. You're not going to ask me what *they* are—the Three Signs of Being?

Garrard No? Why—what are they?

Mrs Rogers I was afraid you might want to know that. Because the only one I can remember is the Four Noble Truths.

Garrard Twelve spokes of this. Three wheels of that. Sounds like a building contract.

Mrs Rogers (*stroking his head*) Then you go through the Four Stages of initiation, which is when you're freeing yourself from the Ten Fetters. The only one of the Ten Fetters I can remember is the last one, which is Ignorance, and I can remember that because it's also the first of the Twelve Spokes of the Wheel of Life.

Garrard is asleep. She stops stroking his hair, and gazes at him. There is the sound of a distant explosion, like the explosions at the beginning of the evening, but louder. Garrard wakes. Mrs Rogers touches his hand, then goes to the window to look out. Garrard leans backwards over the edge of the sofa to reach Mrs Rogers's handbag. He opens it and takes out the torn scraps of paper; but when he straightens up he begins to rub the left-hand side of his chest, in great pain. He drops the scraps of paper. He gives a little gasp at each breath. Mrs Rogers hears this, and turns to look. She moves to Garrard and stands motionless, gazing at him. He looks up at her, then back at the floor, absorbed in himself. He shakes his

*head, then continues to shake it. She goes to the telephone and dials
a single digit*

Garrard No . . . no . . . no . . . It's not that . . .

Mrs Rogers (*into the telephone, calmly*) This is Room 1207.
Will you please call an ambulance?

Garrard (*to himself*) Not that—not that . . .

Mrs Rogers (*into the telephone*) 1207, yes . . . Garrard . . .
G-A-R-R-A-R-D.

Garrard (*to himself*) No . . . no . . . no . . .

Mrs Rogers (*into the telephone*) That's right . . . Thank you . . .
And please—quickly. (*She puts the telephone down*)

Garrard Not that . . . Not that . . . It's just . . . Oh . . . It hurts . . .

She kneels in front of him and takes his hand

Hurts to breathe . . . Can't breathe . . . (*He takes his hand away
and rubs his eyes*) What, not saying anything?

She takes his hand again

Say something to me.

She puts her head down and kisses his hand

What, nothing to say?

She strokes his hand

Tom, Tom—get Tom here.

*She stands up, and hesitates for a moment, looking down at her
dressing-gown. Then she goes to the telephone and dials two digits*

Can't have a day off now. Get this business with Davis fixed.
Board meeting on Tuesday. Get up, get the plane—meeting in
Manchester at lunch-time. No, wait, Tom could do Man-
chester . . . Get Ian Weatherall out to stand in for Tom . . .

Mrs Rogers (*into the telephone*) Oh, Mr Olley, I'm sorry to wake
you. Could you come up to Mr Garrard's room? . . . It's
Mrs Rogers . . . Mr Garrard's not very well . . . Thank you . . .
(*She puts the telephone down and returns to Garrard*)

Garrard Coming, is he?

Mrs Rogers Yes.

Garrard He can do Manchester. I'll get Ian Weatherall out to
take over from Tom . . .

Mrs Rogers Sh. Sh.
Garrard Ring Ian, tell him to get on a plane.
Mrs Rogers If you're not better in the morning.
Garrard Get Frank up here, then. Frank'll have to run this lot
   till Ian arrives.
Mrs Rogers We'll tell him in the morning.
Garrard Oh . . . oh . . . so what, you think it's heart, do you?
Mrs Rogers I'm sure it's not.
Garrard What then, something I've eaten?
Mrs Rogers I expect so.
Garrard Not heart, is it?
Mrs Rogers No, no, no.
Garrard Can't take time off now.
Mrs Rogers Don't fret.
Garrard Not going to die, am I?
Mrs Rogers I won't let you.
Garrard What do you think—couldn't be heart, could it?
Mrs Rogers Sh.
Garrard Where's the ambulance, then? Where's Tom? Quick,
   get Frank up here.
Mrs Rogers In the morning.
Garrard Ring him, ring him.
Mrs Rogers Shall I sing to you?
Garrard Ring him, ring him, ring him!

Mrs Rogers goes to the telephone and dials two digits

   What will they do if it's heart? Won't keep me here, will they?
   They'll fly me back? I've got to be in range of the office. Can't
   keep waiting for calls to London all the time.
Mrs Rogers (*into the telephone*) Oh, Mr Prosser, I'm sorry to
   wake you. Could you come up to Mr Garrard's room? He's
   not feeling too good . . . No, but he wants to make arrangements with you about running the stand . . .

There is a knock at the door

Garrard Open the door!
Mrs Rogers (*into the telephone*) The stand—the *stand*—the
   stand, yes . . .

Urgent knocking at the door

Garrard Door! Door!

Mrs Rogers (*into the telephone*) Quarter-past four, yes—but I'm sorry, I've got to go. (*She puts the telephone down*)

More knocking, as she runs to the door and opens it

> *Olley enters, in a dressing-gown over his pyjamas, but fully awake, alarmed and breathless*

Olley John?

Garrard It's happened, Tom.

Olley looks at him, and controls his alarm

Olley Pain, is it?

Garrard Right through my chest. Steel pin. Each time I breathe . . . Oh . . .

Olley Not too good?

Garrard Bad, Tom. Very bad.

Olley looks at Mrs Rogers

Mrs Rogers I've sent for the ambulance.

Olley He'll get cold like that. Run and fetch him his dressing-gown.

She hesitates, glancing fleetingly down at the dressing-gown

Oh.

Mrs Rogers I'll find something.

> *Mrs Rogers exits into the bedroom*

Olley sits down next to Garrard and puts a hand on his arm

Garrard Well, you warned me often enough.

Olley John, it's probably not what you think.

Garrard No, it's heart, Tom. I know that.

Olley Indigestion can sometimes get you just . . .

Garrard Heart, heart, heart.

Olley I can feel mine pounding. Didn't wait for the lift.

Garrard You told me, didn't you, Tom?

> *Mrs Rogers enters with the duvet from the bed. She puts it round Garrard's shoulders*

Tom . . .

Olley Sh. Just take it easy.

Garrard Tom ... (*He takes Olley's hand, and holds it very tightly*) Tom ... Tom ...

Olley (*to Mrs Rogers, gently*) Why don't you go and put something on?

Mrs Rogers hesitates for a moment, looking helplessly at Garrard, then goes into the bedroom

Garrard (*starting to weep*) I'm going to die.

Olley Not you, John. Not your style. Not the dying type.

Garrard I'm going to die.

Olley I'll die before you, John. Want to bet on it?

Garrard I should have listened to you, Tom. But what did you want me to do? You wanted me to do nothing!

Olley You couldn't do nothing.

Garrard What? Sit and look at the ceiling all day? I couldn't do it.

Olley Of course not.

Garrard (*weeping*) Don't want to die, Tom. *Can't* die. Can't die *now*.

Olley Not your turn today, John.

Garrard What'll it be like, Tom?

Olley It'll be all right, when it happens. You'll be ready for it.

Garrard And what, it'll be just—darkness?

Olley No, not darkness.

Garrard What, then?

Olley Like coming out of darkness. Like coming into the light.

Garrard Be nothing, won't it, Tom. Just suddenly—nothing.

Olley There'll be something.

Garrard Nothing. Just nothing more. Nothing more ever.

Pause. Garrard sighs. The panic has subsided into dejection

All nothing, really, though. You keep juggling it, you keep it all up in the air, it looks as solid as houses. Take your eyes off it for a moment, and it's gone, it's nothing

Mrs Rogers enters, dressed

Olley (*to Mrs Rogers*) Give them another ring.

Mrs Rogers dials a single digit

Garrard Nothing. Black nothing.

Mrs Rogers (*into the telephone*) We asked for an ambulance . . .
    Would you? Thank you . . . (*She waits*)
Garrard Listen, Tom . . .
Olley Sh. Only make it worse if you keep worrying, John.
Garrard No, listen, listen.
Olley It'll be all right in the end, John. I promise you.
Garrard No, this is important. You'll have to do that meeting in
    Manchester for me.
Olley Yes, yes, yes . . .

There is a knock at the door. Mrs Rogers puts the receiver down
beside the telephone and runs to open the door

> *Prosser enters. He is wearing a raincoat over his pyjamas, and a*
> *sock on one foot. He is thick-headed and confused. He leaves the*
> *door slightly open*

Prosser Sorry. Trying to find the other sock.
Olley Frank . . .
Prosser What's up?
Olley Nothing's up.
Prosser Meeting? Some kind of meeting?
Mrs Rogers (*to Olley*) Mr Garrard asked me to ring Mr Prosser.
    (*Into the telephone*) Hello . . .? (*Nothing. She waits*)
Prosser Something about the stand. Arrangements on the
    stand.
Olley It's John. He's not feeling too good.
Garrard I'm dying, Frank.
Olley No, you're not, John. Now come on.
Garrard Heart.
Olley It may be your heart.
Garrard My heart's gone, Frank.
Olley We don't know yet.
Garrard Can't breathe.
Olley Sh.

Prosser continues staring at the two of them for some moments,
then turns to the display

Prosser And what's wrong with the stand?
Olley (*to Mrs Rogers*) What's all this about the stand?
Garrard Doesn't matter. Doesn't matter.

Mrs Rogers (*into the telephone*) Hello ... I see ... I see ...
Thank you. But you will keep trying them? ... Yes ...
Thank you. (*She puts the telephone down*) There's been some
kind of bomb incident somewhere. We may have to wait a few
minutes for the ambulance. They're trying to get us a doctor.
The stand? Mr Garrard wanted to talk to Mr Prosser about
running the stand until Mr Weatherall arrived. He wanted
Mr Weatherall to come out and take over from you while you
fly back to Manchester and do his meeting with the Department
of Industry.

Olley I see.

Prosser I haven't got my watch.

Mrs Rogers Four twenty-five.

Prosser You mean, go now?

Olley What?

Prosser Fly back to Manchester now?

Olley Not now. Not you. Frank, have you been on the grog?

Prosser Verhaeren wouldn't go to bed.

Mrs Rogers Mr Prosser was up here at midnight singing
Beethoven symphonies.

Garrard Telling us the point of it all.

Olley The point of all what?

Garrard Everything. Life.

Olley Oh. (*To Prosser*) And what *was* the point of it all?

Prosser Sorry?

Garrard Come on, Frank, sing up.

Olley Sing?

Garrard He sings it.

Olley Sings what?

Garrard (*impatiently*) The point. He sings the point. He tells you
what the point is by singing it. Come on, Frank.

Olley You want him to *sing?* What—*now?*

Garrard If he knows the point of it all, Tom, then let's not sit
around in misery, let's hear it.

Olley But you don't like music.

Garrard I don't like sitting here wrapped in an eiderdown waiting
to die.

Olley You're not waiting to die.

Garrard We're all waiting to die. So sing, sing, sing, sing, sing.

Olley All right, then, Frank. Sing it and get it over with.

Prosser (*appalled*) Sing what?

Olley Whatever you were singing before.

Mrs Rogers Beethoven symphonies.

Prosser What, the Seventh? (*He opens his mouth, but then closes it again*) I've forgotten how it goes.

Olley Sing us another one, then. Anything. Couple of bars.

Prosser (*thinking*) This is ridiculous. Can't think of a single note in any of them. I know them all backwards . . .! Oh, yes. (*He sings a note, then stops*) Oh, no.

Garrard Go on, go on.

Prosser (*awkwardly*) Well, it's the Eroica. It's the Funeral March.

Olley Frank, pull yourself together, will you?

Prosser No, I know. (*Singing*) *Freude, schöner Götterfunken* . . . Sorry . . . *Freude, schöner Götterfunken* . . . I can't get it to go up in the right place . . .

Olley What is it?

Prosser It's the Ninth—the Hymn to Joy . . .

Prosser tries again. This time, with the help of Olley and Mrs Rogers, he gets it going right, and sings on with more and more voice, hammering out the time on the back of a chair. Olley puts his head in his hand and covers his eyes. Garrard continues to rub his chest and grimace with pain

> *Freude, schöner Götterfunken,*
> *Tochter aus Elysium,*
> *Wir betreten feuertrunken,*
> *Himmlische, dein Heiligtum.*

The Doctor enters through the open door. He is German, a youngish, unsmiling man with long hair. He looks at a card he is holding

Olley and Mrs Rogers stop humming. Prosser sings on alone, with his eyes closed

> *Deine Zauber binden wieder,*
> *Was die Mode streng geteilt,*
> *Alle Menschen werden Brüder . . .*

Prosser sees the Doctor, and stops

Doctor English?

Mrs Rogers Yes.
Prosser Sorry.
Doctor This is the patient?
Olley Mr Garrard.
Mrs Rogers Would you like us to go?

The Doctor sits beside Garrard, in Olley's place, and takes Garrard's wrist

Doctor Pain, yes?
Garrard Heart. Heart. They've been telling me for years.
Doctor Bad pain?
Garrard Bad pain, yes. Very bad. Can't breathe.
Doctor Can't breathe? Why can't you breathe?
Garrard Hurts.
Doctor Hurts when you breathe?
Garrard Yes.
Doctor Where?
Garrard Here.
Doctor On the left?
Garrard Yes. In the heart.
Doctor Front? Back?
Garrard Right through.
Doctor What sort of pain?
Garrard Like a knife. Right through my chest.
Doctor Like a knife?
Garrard Like being stabbed, each time I breathe.
Doctor Nothing here?
Garrard No.
Doctor Nor here?
Garrard No.
Doctor Only on the left?
Garrard Yes.
Doctor When did the pain start?
Garrard Just now.
Mrs Rogers About quarter of an hour ago.
Doctor Suddenly?
Garrard Just like that.
Doctor Before this—any trouble?
Garrard They've been warning me for years.
Doctor But some pain here before?

Garrard No.
Doctor Have you been making some strong exercise?
Garrard No.
Mrs Rogers Well . . .
Garrard Oh. Well . . .
Olley Frank and I'll wait in the corridor.
Prosser What?
Olley Come on.

Olley and Prosser exit

Doctor You're his wife?
Mrs Rogers No.
Doctor So this was some . . . unusual strong exercise?
Mrs Rogers Well . . .
Garrard Yes.

Pause. The Doctor thinks

Mrs Rogers Shall I wait outside?
Doctor No, no. (*To Garrard, indicating the duvet*) Off, please.

Garrard takes off the duvet

Turn round.

Garrard turns, at the Doctor's indication, and presents his back for inspection. The Doctor feels carefully along the middle section of the spine. Suddenly Garrard lets out a sharp cry of pain

There?
Garrard Yes.
Doctor That's the pain?
Garrard Yes.
Doctor And it's just—

He presses again, with the same result

—there.
Garrard So what, am I fit to travel? I can't stay here. I've got to get back to the office.
Doctor (*unlacing his right shoe*) Lie down.
Garrard Lie down?
Doctor On the floor.
Garrard What? What's this?

Doctor (*nodding at the floor*) Lie, please.

Garrard gets down on to it, very anxious, and lies on his back

Garrard What? What? What's happening?
Doctor Turn over.
Garrard (*turning over on to his stomach*) This way? What's going on?

The Doctor sets his stockinged foot in the middle of Garrard's spine, and puts his weight on it. There is a loud, sharp crack, and Garrard screams

Doctor Stand up.

Garrard climbs shakily to his feet, holding both chest and back

Breathe. More, more . . .
Garrard The pain's gone!
Doctor (*replacing his shoe*) All right?
Garrard Nothing there at all!
Doctor So, one hundred and twenty marks.
Garrard And what, you mean it's all fixed?
Doctor If you have some more pain in the next twenty-four hours, call this number, and you must have an electrocardiogram. But I think there will be no more pain now.
Mrs Rogers It wasn't his heart?
Doctor A disc out of place.
Garrard In my back?
Doctor People quite often make this mistake. (*To Mrs Rogers*) You called the ambulance?

Mrs Rogers nods, unable to speak. The Doctor picks up the telephone and dials a single digit

Mrs Rogers I'm sorry. I'll get the money. (*She goes to the drawer of her desk*)
Doctor You thought you should be going to die?
Garrard Yes.
Doctor (*giving a slight laugh*) Now you must get used to remain alive again. (*Into the telephone*) Zwölfhundertsieben. Doktor Sorge. Bitte, bestellen Sie den Krankenwagen ab . . . Danke. (*He puts the telephone down*) You work hard?

Garrard shrugs

Mrs Rogers He never stops.

Doctor You worry about your work?

Garrard Not particularly.

Mrs Rogers Work and worry about work—that's his entire life. (*She gives the Doctor the money*)

Doctor So tomorrow, next week—who knows?—maybe you will have a real heart attack. The pain will be here, in the middle. It won't be like a knife. It will be like ... (*He demonstrates, pushing his clenched fists towards each other*)

Mrs Rogers A vice.

Doctor And you're right—this is how half of all people die. (*He writes out a receipt for the money*)

Garrard So what, you're a pretty good doctor, are you?

Doctor I once was specialized in orthopaedic work. I made something with osteopathy. Quite fortunate for you, I think. (*He hands over the receipt, gives a bleak smile, and opens the door to leave*)

Garrard So what happened? Why are you doing night calls if you're a specialist?

Doctor I was specialized in the D.D.R.—in East Germany. Now since three years I am living in the Federal Republic, and it's very difficult. Too many doctors. I must work at night, as if I was Turkish.

Olley and Prosser enter cautiously, Olley miming a tap on the open door. They gaze in amazement at Garrard

Garrard East Germany? What, still got contacts there, have you? We want to open up in Eastern Europe with all this range—demountable walls, Bürolandschaft—it's a complete internal wall system. Anyone you know who might be useful?

Doctor I know some people in the hospitals.

Garrard We sell to hospitals.

Doctor I have some friends in certain government departments.

Garrard I mean, this would be a business proposition as far as you're concerned.

Doctor Of course. Also it will be quite amusing. Give me this card for one moment. (*He writes on it*) Call me tomorrow at this number. Between six and eight. Really, this will be very funny. You can bring my friends some Levis and some records of unsuitable music, and all these things.

Garrard Right. And I'll just give you my ... (*He realizes that he has no card on him in his present attire. To Olley and Prosser*) Card.

Olley What?

Garrard Card, card.

Olley and Prosser pat their pyjama and raincoat pockets helplessly

(*To the Doctor*) Take some of this, anyway. (*He goes to the small table at the back of the display, turns on the lamp and picks up a random handful of literature, which he gives to the Doctor*) It's all in here. Give you an idea.

Doctor Anyway, you'll call me.

Garrard Between six and eight.

Doctor We will make something together. (*He shakes Garrard's hand*)

Garrard Been a pleasure.

The Doctor exits

(*To Olley*) Worth following up, anyway. Might just give us an alternative to Horvath. What do you think—East Germany—could be a better start than Hungary, couldn't it?

Olley John, just a moment. I think Frank and I have missed a stage or two here.

Garrard Refugee. East Germany. Got contacts there.

Olley John, are you now—all right?

Garrard What? Oh, yes, fine.

Olley Because when we last saw you, two minutes ago, if you remember, you were slightly under the weather.

Garrard Fine, fine, fine.

Prosser We were standing out there, and there was this terrible scream ...

Olley We thought you must have ... Well, we thought you must still have been feeling a little seedy.

Garrard Slipped disc. He fixed it. Did you get anything out of your dinner with Goetz?

Olley Hold on. It *wasn't* a heart attack?

Garrard Back, back.

Olley And you're no longer in pain?

Garrard I'm fine. Is Goetz going to give us anything or not?

Olley John—I've half a mind to take hold of you and shake you until you *do* have a heart attack.

Garrard (*thinking*) Yes. Sorry, Tom. Thanks. Shan't forget it.

Olley I didn't mean that.

Garrard No, it's just that since he was from East Germany . . .

Olley No, I mean we've all had a bit of a fright, John.

Garrard Yes, but since he did just happen to have contacts in East Germany . . .

Olley We're all very fond of you.

Pause. Garrard nods, looking at the floor

> We like you. You see? We're quite pleased to find you're not dying after all. We just need a moment or two to take it in. And we're all a bit bloody angry with ourselves because our hearts have gone thump thump thump for nothing. People get upset, you know, when things happen to someone they love. (*Pause*) You *shit*. (*Pause*) I'll tell you about Goetz in the morning.

> *Olley exits*

Garrard What time's Verhaeren coming?

Prosser I think he said nine.

Garrard Get some sleep.

Prosser Yes. And the stand . . .

Garrard What?

Prosser The stand's all right?

Garrard Yes, yes, yes.

> *Prosser exits*

Mrs Rogers I'm sorry. I shall have to sit down. (*She sits*) My legs are shaking. I'm sorry. (*She starts to cry*)

Garrard What? What?

She shakes her head

> You're shivering.

Mrs Rogers I'm sorry.

Garrard Put this round you. (*He drapes her in the duvet*) Get you some brandy.

She shakes her head

> Get the doctor back for *you*.

She stops crying, and gives a small laugh

Mrs Rogers Yes. That's all I need. Someone to walk over me.

Garrard What, you mean I have? Bit embarrassing, was it? Never look Tom in the eye again?

Pause. She takes his hand. He sits beside her and pats her arm

Mrs Rogers When I turned round and saw you sitting here, and you were holding your chest, and you had that look on your face . . .

Garrard I was all right till I saw the look on *your* face.

Mrs Rogers You were so frightened. (*Pause*) I saw my father when he was dying. He took my hand and held it. Just looked at me and held my hand in both of his. Held it and held it. I wanted to run out of the room. I had to pretend to myself that my hand didn't belong to me. I had to think of it lying there on the covers like something dead. He'd been ill for a long time. I was sixteen. (*Pause*) Didn't want me, did you?

Garrard Anyway, it never happened.

Mrs Rogers It will one day.

Garrard You won't be there.

Mrs Rogers No, I shan't be there. (*She rises, picks up the bear, and looks round the room*) I suppose I shall be working at that desk again in a few hours. It'll be just another day.

Garrard Stay if you want to.

She shakes her head

Dinner one night when we get back.

Mrs Rogers (*not believing it*) Yes.

Garrard When you're not seeing your pal.

Mrs Rogers That would be nice.

Garrard Get some sleep.

Mrs Rogers Yes. I suppose I should say thank you for a lovely evening.

Garrard And what—a raindrop?

Mrs Rogers (*handing him the torn scraps of paper from her bag*) In a clear sky.

Mrs Rogers exits

Garrard goes slowly to the chair where he was sitting earlier. He drops the paper then crumples into the chair and sits with his head bowed—nothing. There is a tap at the door. Garrard hears it, but does not move. Another tap. Wearily, Garrard gets up and opens the door. Olley stands on the threshold

Olley Better tell you now, hadn't I? About Goetz. Never sleep
if I don't, will you.

*Garrard returns to his chair and sits down as before. Olley comes
into the room and closes the door*

Sorry I snapped. Shouldn't have done that. Sorry.

Pause. Garrard nods

That's really what I came to say, of course. *I* shouldn't have
slept otherwise. Anyway, Goetz. It's thirty-minute fire-walling
for his school chemistry labs. I think I've sold him. I'd guess
about eight thousand square metres.

Pause. Garrard nods

Now you know. So now it's as cold as cold turkey, isn't it.

Pause. Olley moves to Garrard

Come on, John. Get to bed. Get some sleep. I'm going to
stand over you. Cluck cluck cluck, like a mother chicken. Off
you go.

*Olley touches Garrard's shoulder. Garrard sighs, and gets to his
feet. He gazes at Olley*

Got to close the works down sometimes, John. Even you.

*Garrard rests his forehead on Olley's shoulder. Olley puts his arm
round him*

*Then Garrard straightens up, walks slowly into the bedroom, nods
at Olley from the threshold, and closes the door*

*Olley notices the scraps of paper lying where Garrard dropped
them. He picks them up, looks at them, then stiffens in irritation.
He goes and turns off the lights at the main door. He goes through
the display to the table behind, where the table lamp is still lit.
For a moment he is silhouetted by the light against the obscured
glass screen in one of the movable elements. Then the lamp is
switched off*

Darkness. A strange, gentle sound

The lights come up on the display. Prosser is sitting on the edge of a chair, wearing his ordinary suit, and holding a folded raincoat and a bunch of flowers

> *Hewlett enters through one of the doors in the display. He is also carrying a folded coat and flowers*

Prosser puts a warning finger to his lips

Prosser (*keeping his voice down*) He's still asleep. We have to wait until visiting time.

Hewlett nods and closes the door with care. He sits down on the edge of another chair

> He couldn't be in a better place, though. Beautiful. Very peaceful in this evening light. Woods quietly sinking into shadow. Quiet gravel on the paths. I think he'll be happy here. He always wanted deep lawns where profound deer gathered towards nightfall.

Hewlett tries to conceal his tears

> Come on, now. He'd want us to be deep. Deep and golden.

> *Mrs Rogers enters through one of the doors in the display, wearing a white overall*

Prosser and Hewlett stand up

Mrs Rogers Good evening. Are you the immediate family?
Prosser How is he, Doctor?
Mrs Rogers As well as can be expected. The whole frontal has undergone a series of, and the right-hand part of the upper is particularly.
Prosser I see. Of course.
Mrs Rogers I just want to warn you that you may find him slightly, and also a little, perhaps.
Prosser I understand. Thank you.
Mrs Rogers I'll bring him in, then.

She unbolts one of the moving panels in the display, and revolves it to reveal an upright open coffin. Inside the coffin is an ancient, swaddled, mummified figure, its face shrouded and obscure

Prosser Hello, John!

Hewlett Hello, Mr Garrard!

Prosser How goes it, then?

Hewlett You're looking well!

Prosser I'm the one who ought to be lying there you know!

Hewlett Looking after you, are they?

Prosser I don't know—some people have all the luck.

Hewlett Don't you talk, Mr Garrard. Mustn't tire yourself.

Prosser Let's think. What's been happening in the office?

Hewlett We got into East Anglia.

Prosser Oh, yes, we got into East Anglia, John.

Hewlett Ian Weatherall flew out from Paddington.

Prosser Oh, and you remember Mrs Rogers? Tom's secretary? I think she's having a bit of a thing with John Garrard. Remember John Garrard?

Hewlett John Garrard! I wonder what happened to him?

Prosser I think someone told me he became a Buddhist. Gave everything up. Went off in search of nirvana.

Mrs Rogers *(to Hewlett)* You want nirvana? It's through here . . .

Hewlett We ought to have a look at nirvana now we're here.

Mrs Rogers opens one of the doors in the display and leads Hewlett through

Prosser Because what you're looking for, if you're looking for nirvana, is a fully integrated system . . . (*He goes out through another door*)

Hewlett (*enters by a third door*) . . . where you are part of the system and the system is part of you.

From now on salesmen appear and disappear, demonstrating the display, as at the beginning of Act I, by shifting all the movable panels. Each is absorbed by his own activity

The mummified figure remains visible as the axis of all this activity

Olley Because what we offer is four basic truths, and as you turn this truth round you can see that what it consists of is simply this . . .

Anni It's just an eightfold way, and the first fold, which is this wall here . . .

Hewlett . . . is built entirely out of the four basic truths . . .

Prosser . . . and the second fold has a laminated core consisting of the five soundproof states of consciousness.

Mrs Rogers ... of which the four basic truths are the same as the third of the four subsidiary companies in the human components division ...

Olley ... and the fourth of which is the knowledge that the first two are none other than the four basic doors ...

Corpse Wait! (*It steps forward from its coffin, its face still not quite visible, but its voice the voice of Garrard*)

Everyone freezes

So what, we're meeting Verhaeren at nine?

The dream collapses in broken light and noise. Darkness

A knock at the door. Subdued daylight comes slowly up on the room, filtered through the drawn curtains. The display is uninhabited, and its evolutions have left it exactly as it was before. Another knock

Mrs Rogers enters, fresh and trim for the day's work, and carrying letters and newspapers. Garrard enters from the bedroom, dressed, stuffing papers into his overnight bag

Garrard Taxi, get me a taxi. I'm on the ten forty-five Manchester.

Mrs Rogers Good morning, Mr Garrard. I'll leave the door on the latch for everyone, shall I? (*She goes to the telephone and dials a single digit, then watches him as he hurries to the window and flings open the curtains*)

Garrard Where's Tom? Verhaeren's going to be here at nine. Tom'll have to deal with him. I can't stay more than ten minutes. Give Tom a ring—get him up here.

Hewlett enters

Hewlett Good morning, Mr Garrard.

Garrard (*to Mrs Rogers*) No, taxi, taxi. (*To Hewlett*) You run down and fetch Tom. Tell him Verhaeren's going to be here any minute.

Hewlett exits

Tell them we want the taxi *now*. This is the number for that doctor. Tom'll have to ring him—between six and eight, tell him. This is a note for Horvath. It's very rough. Knock it into shape as you type it out. Don't let Horvath near Tom. If he rings ...

Mrs Rogers Sorry . . . (*Into the telephone*) Room One-two-oh-seven. Could we have a taxi, please? For the airport.
Garrard Now.
Mrs Rogers Now, please. It is urgent . . . Thank you. (*She puts the telephone down*)
Garrard If he rings, if Horvath rings—

Anni enters. She stops at the sight of them together

Anni Oh . . . !
Garrard (*to Mrs Rogers*) —go downstairs and deal with him yourself. (*To Anni*) What?
Anni I'm so sorry!
Garrard What? What do you want?
Anni The door was open . . .
Garrard (*oblivious*) Down there on the floor, aren't you?
Anni Ten o'clock. First I need some more publicity things (*She indicates the material on the stand*)
Garrard (*to Mrs Rogers*) If he rings before I've left, tell him to wait downstairs, I'll see him there. (*To Anni*) Come on, then.

Anni goes to the display and begins to help herself to leaflets, but looks curiously all the time at Garrard and Mrs Rogers

(*To Mrs Rogers*) If he just walks in and Tom gets hold of him, you'll have to use your initiative, you'll have to see him out afterwards. But whatever you do make sure he doesn't leave without that note.

Prosser enters, still slightly under the weather, and acting up to it

Prosser Good morning. I think.
Garrard All right, you can look after Verhaeren. Handle Verhaeren, can you, Frank?
Prosser Expert. Already handled him into a taxi. Out of a taxi. Through a revolving door.
Garrard Right, you handle Verhaeren. First just you run downstairs . . .
Anni *Run* downstairs?
Garrard Get Tom up here, fetch Colin Hewlett back.

Prosser opens the door, and runs humorously straight into Verhaeren, who is standing on the threshold. He reels back,

*dazed. Verhaeren, in the best of health, bursts out laughing at the
sight of him, and puts his arm round Prosser's shoulders*

Anni Oh, Mr Verhaeren! You see what you've made with poor
Frank?

Verhaeren puts his other arm round Anni

Prosser How are you this morning, then, Mr Verhaeren?
Verhaeren (*laughing*) Why? What's wrong?
Anni Look! He's very good!
Garrard (*impatiently*) Right, then . . .
Prosser This is John Garrard, our Managing Director.
Verhaeren (*giving Garrard a genial handshake*) How do you do?
Garrard Nice to meet you. Right, then, sound reduction. That
the problem? Don't want to rush you, but I've got a plane to
catch. (*To Mrs Rogers*) That taxi there yet?
Mrs Rogers (*with a start, although she is staring straight at him*)
Sorry?
Garrard What?
Mrs Rogers I didn't . . .
Garrard What are you on about?
Mrs Rogers Nothing . . . (*She busies herself in confusion with the
stuff on her desk*)
Garrard (*to Verhaeren*) Right. So the standard core, that's inert
European flaxboard, and that'll give you a sound reduction of
thirty-two dB. But if you want more you can have it. This
unit, for instance . . .

Shaw enters

Shaw Look at him, though. Not nine yet, and hard at it already!
Garrard I'm with a customer, Ted.
Shaw No, but that's the way all these big men do it, isn't it,
Frank?
Garrard (*to Verhaeren*) Identical exterior, but the Firemode core
in plasterboard and steel, and that'll take you up to forty-seven
dB . . .
Shaw Start work while the rest of us are still in dreamland.
Garrard (*to Verhaeren*) And if you like to come round here . . .
(*To Mrs Rogers, who is standing gazing at him again*) Ring
them, then, ring them!

Mrs Rogers Sorry. (*She picks up the telephone*)

Garrard All got a day's work to do.

Mrs Rogers Yes. (*She dials*)

Shaw (*to Prosser*) No, but it's true. Seven-thirty this morning, knock on my door, and who is it?—it's Peter Davis.

Garrard Peter Davis?

Shaw You attend to your customer, John.

Garrard (*to Verhaeren*) This is a core we supply to order, and it'll give you fifty-one dB . . . (*To Shaw*) So what, he's selling you?

Shaw On the contrary, John, on the contrary.

Hewlett enters

I think he's promoting me.

Hewlett Mr Garrard . . .

Garrard Promoting you?

Hewlett I'm sorry.

Shaw From what he hinted.

Garrard How? Where?

Shaw Something about a Building Components Division.

Garrard What? What? What did he say about it?

Shaw (*enjoying taking his time*) I think young Colin here is trying to sell you some partitions.

Hewlett No, sorry, it's just I can't find Mr Olley anywhere.

Garrard End up doing everything yourself in this world. (*To Shaw*) Hold on for two minutes. I want to hear the end of this story. (*To Verhaeren*) Fifty-one decibels, right? (*To Hewlett*) Look in the street, see if he's taking a stroll. (*To Verhaeren*) What that means is total sound isolation, complete privacy, living in a world of your own, no idea what's happening on the other side—until you unlock it, look—seen this, have you?— what the product's all about, and . . .

Garrard turns the element with the obscured glass in it, and reveals Olley. He is sitting in pyjamas and dressing-gown in a high-backed office chair, with one hand still on the light switch. His head is back, his eyes are open, and his jaw is hanging slack. Garrard and Verhaeren stare at him

Mrs Rogers (*into the telephone, with a start*) Sorry? . . . Oh . . .

Yes, I was just going to ask—what was I going to ask?—is the taxi for 1207 there?

Prosser (*to Verhaeren*) I thought you might be interested in this report of our fifty-one dB by the Building Research Centre . . .

Prosser sees Olley. So does Hewlett, as he opens the door to go out

Anni (*to Shaw*) You have eaten peppermints for breakfast.

Shaw Keeping myself fresh and pure for you, my sweetheart . . . What?

Anni has now seen Olley. Shaw turns and sees him as well

Mrs Rogers (*into the telephone*) Thank you. (*To Garrard*) Mr Garrard, the taxi is . . . (*She sees Olley*)

Everyone is now standing stock still, gazing at the body. Garrard unwillingly puts out his hand, and touches Olley's hand for an instant

Garrard Cold as putty.

Garrard takes Olley by the shoulders, and gently pulls him forward. The head flops on to the chest. Garrard lowers him until the head is resting, face concealed, on the desk he is sitting at. He closes the wall element in front of him again

Garrard walks out through the main door

Pause

Shaw (*keeping his voice low*) Heart?

Prosser I don't know.

Hewlett Doctor. Or someone. Get someone.

Prosser In a minute. No hurry.

Shaw What about John?

Prosser Yes. I'll go.

Mrs Rogers Leave him. Leave him. He won't want you. He won't want anyone.

Pause

Verhaeren I am sorry.

Prosser He was a fine man.

Shaw I can't believe it.

Anni starts to cry. No-one comforts her

Verhaeren Did he have a warning? Trouble before?
Prosser Not as far as I know. (*To Mrs Rogers*) Did he?

Mrs Rogers shakes her head, dazed

Can't take it in, can you? I know you two used to squabble, but . . .
Mrs Rogers I was thinking of Mr Garrard.
Shaw Yes, poor John. He's going to take this very hard.
Prosser Ironic, really, isn't it? Tom was always warning him. (*To Mrs Rogers*) And when you think he was up here holding Garrard's hand . . . (*To the others*) Middle of the night. Garrard thought he was going to die.
Shaw Known each other for, what, thirty years?
Prosser Thirty-two. Tom was just saying yesterday. Met in a demob centre after the war, didn't they?
Shaw Somebody's office, that was the story. Both going after the same job. Wearing exactly the same demob suit, same hat, same tie. So Tom starts to laugh, and John says, "What? What? What?" Because of course being John he can't see it.
Prosser Put their gratuities together to start the firm. Wasn't that it?
Shaw Going to be a real shock for John, this.
Prosser Coincidence, though, isn't it, Garrard getting us all up here in the night. Really scared old Tom. Telling me outside. Came running up three flights of stairs expecting to find John dead.
Shaw Not such a coincidence, then, was it?

Pause. They look at each other

Prosser Put it like that . . . Bit of a creaser for John, when you think about it.

Garrard enters. They all look at him, not knowing what to say. He thinks

Verhaeren I should like to offer you my sympathy.
Shaw We're all very sad about this, John.
Prosser We know how you must feel.

Garrard Hold on. (*To Mrs Rogers*) Get me on the eleven-forty London. Will she be in this morning? Jean—his wife? Ring Ian and tell him he'll have to do the meeting in Manchester.

Mrs Rogers just gazes at him helplessly

Verhaeren I must go away and leave you to . . .

Garrard Wait, wait. Frank'll deal with you. Frank . . .? (*To Mrs Rogers*) And tell him not to give way on floor area—we must have thirty thousand square feet or the site's useless. Then get on to the British consul and find out how we get the body home—what's the drill—will they need to have an inquest. Get on to them first of all, before we notify anyone here.

Prosser John . . .

Garrard (*to Prosser*) You hold the fort here this morning. I'll come straight back from London, as soon as I've spoken to Jean. Get Ian out here tomorrow . . .

The telephone rings. Mrs Rogers picks it up

Mrs Rogers (*into the telephone*) Hello . . .? Oh . . . yes . . . (*She waits to speak to Garrard*)

Garrard (*to Prosser*) Oh, and Goetz—Tom reckoned he'd got somewhere with him. You'd better ring him and pick up the threads.

Shaw John, if there's anything I can do . . .

Garrard Building Components Division? So what, he was saying he'd make you Managing Director? Is that it?

Shaw We'll talk about that some other time, shall we, John?

Garrard (*to Mrs Rogers*) Make an appointment for me to see Peter Davis—lunchtime—before I get the plane back. If they try and tell you he's busy say we've got a bereavement in the firm.

Mrs Rogers (*holding the receiver*) It's Dr Horvath. He's downstairs. I'll put him off, shall I?

Garrard What for? No problem there now. Get him up here.

Mrs Rogers (*into the phone*) Will you come up, Dr Horvath . . .?

Garrard And the taxi?

Mrs Rogers (*putting the telephone down*) It's waiting.

Garrard What else? (*He stands still, eyes closed, hand to head, older than before*)

Prosser (*close to tears*) Can't believe he won't just suddenly walk
through that door, though. One of his big smiles all over his
face. All some kind of mistake. Poor bloody Tom. He was a
good man. Kind man. Man of great sweetness, great ... I
don't know how we're all going to get by without him.

Anni cries

Garrard Yes. Could Ian do the job? I suppose you'd be in the
running for it, would you?

Prosser (*gently*) John, for God's sake—I know how this is hitting
you ...

Mrs Rogers (*quietly*) Leave him. He doesn't want anyone.

Prosser But look, it's no good blaming ourselves. I mean, I'm
not religious, or anything ... but *he* was, and I suppose whatever
it's like for the rest of us we have to feel that for him it's ...
some kind of rest, some kind of peace ...

Garrard (*abstractedly*) Rest ... peace ... Yes, and we'll be all
bloody week getting it sorted out, getting his body back.

*Silence. They are all chilled and uneasy at his attitude. He gazes
abstractedly at the display*

Mrs Rogers I just wish it had been me.

Silence

Garrard All standing here, nothing to do. Go crazy. Get this
display straight ...

Garrard starts to rearrange the display. No-one else moves

CURTAIN

FURNITURE AND PROPERTY LIST

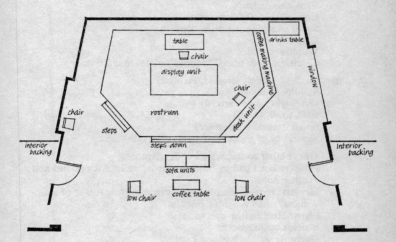

ACT I

On stage: **ROSTRUM:**

Display stand: sections of apparently solid walling finished in veneered panels, sections of which can be moved and turned into new positions. In centre section is a panel of obscured glass

Small table (above C panel of display). *On it:* writing materials, leaflets, various papers, table lamp

Shelf. *On it:* coffee-making machine, cups, saucers, spoons, sugar basin

Desk unit. *On it:* telephone, leaflets, price lists, business literature, writing materials, order books, ashtray. *In drawer:* German money. *Under it:* sealed box of Beethoven records, wastepaper-basket. *Attached to front:* samples of various wood panels

Small chair behind desk

Small chair at table up C

ROOM AREA:
Drinks. table. *On it:* whisky, gin, vodka, dry and sweet
Martini, sherry, soda syphon, lemon squash, assorted
glasses
Sofa made up of 2 detachable seat units
2 matching chairs
Coffee-table. *On it:* ashtray
Small chair (above main door)
Carpet
Window curtains
Catch, number plate, "Modus" plate on main door

Off stage: Leaflets, (Olley, Prosser, Hewlett)
Shoulder-satchel (Anni)
Overnight bag (Garrard)
Bath towel (Anni)
Small magazine (Garrard)
Several large shopping parcels (Horvath)

Personal: Olley: lapel badge, wallet with snapshots
Prosser: lapel badge, business cards, wallet with pound and
other notes
Hewlett: lapel badge, business cards, watch, folder of snap-
shots, small religious booklet
Shaw: lapel badge, spectacles
Shariq: business card
Garrard: watch, business card
Horvath: card, piece of paper with address
Mrs Rogers: evening handbag, watch

ACT II

Strike: Used glasses and cups
Set   Coffin with swaddled figure (of Garrard) concealed in display
              unit

Off stage: Very large teddy-bear (Mrs Rogers)
Duvet (Mrs Rogers)
Doctor's bag (Doctor)
Folded raincoat, bunch of flowers (Prosser)
Folded raincoat, bunch of flowers (Hewlett)
White overall (Mrs Rogers)
Letters, newspapers (Mrs Rogers)
Overnight bag, papers (Garrard)

Personal Doctor: card, receipt book, pen

LIGHTING PLOT

Property fittings required: wall brackets, table lamp, illuminated
  display signs

ACT I

To open: Brackets and display signs lit
Cue 1   **Garrard:** "Eat, eat, eat . . ."   (Page 55)
         Black-out on set

ACT II

To open: Darkness
Cue 2   **Garrard** switches on main lights   (Page 56)
         Snap on wall brackets

Cue 3   **Garrard** experiments with lights   (Page 56)
         *Snap display lights and brackets on and off,
            finishing with partial lighting from brackets to
            give intimate effect*

Cue 4   **Mrs Rogers** turns off lights   (Page 77)
         *Snag of wall brackets, leaving off-stage bedroom
            strip on; after **Mrs Rogers** exits, take bedroom
            strip off also*

Cue 5   **Garrard** (*off*): ". . . if we get into Eastern
           Europe." (third time)   (Page 77)
         Display lights on

Cue 6   Bedroom door opens   (Page 78)
         Snap off display lights

Cue 7   **Garrard** switches on main lights   (Page 78)
         Snap on wall brackets

Cue 8   **Garrard** goes to small table   (Page 91)
         Switch on table lamp

Cue 9   **Olley** turns off main lights   (Page 94)
         Snap off wall brackets

Cue 10	After **Olley** goes to small table	(Page 94)
	Snap off table lamp to Black-out. Pause. After sound starts snap on display lights	
Cue 11	**"Corpse"** "... we're meeting Verhaeren at nine?"	(Page 97)
	Broken light then black-out, followed, after knock on door, by subdued daylight through drawn curtains	
Cue 12	**Garrard** opens curtains *Bring up to full daylight*	(Page 97)

EFFECTS PLOT

ACT I

Cue 1	**Hewlett** "... you'll see we are offering, ex-stock ..." *Distant explosion*	(Page 2)
Cue 2	**Prosser** "... because we need the business." *Distant explosion*	(Page 5)
Cue 3	**Mrs Rogers** "... walking right back in here ..." *Crash*	(Page 27)

ACT II

Cue 4	**Garrard:** "Come on, come on, come on, come on ..." *Telephone rings*	(Page 67)
Cue 5	As **Mrs Rogers** stops stroking **Garrard's** hair *Distant explosion but louder than previously*	(Page 79)
Cue 6	**Doctor** puts weight on **Garrard's** spine *Loud, sharp crack*	(Page 89)
Cue 7	After table lamp goes off *Strange, gentle sound*	(Page 94)
Cue 8	**"Corpse"** "... we're meeting Verhaeren at nine?" *End of dream 'noise'*	(Page 97)
Cue 9	**Garrard:** "Get Ian out here tomorrow." *Telephone rings*	(Page 103)

MADE AND PRINTED IN GREAT BRITAIN BY
LATIMER TREND & COMPANY LTD PLYMOUTH
MADE IN ENGLAND